# 77 BIBLE STUDIES FOR 21st CENTURY MUMS

# 77 Bible Studies for 21st Century Mums

**MARY PYTCHES**

MONARCH
BOOKS

Mill Hill, London and Grand Rapids, Michigan

First published by Monarch Books in the UK in 2001,
Concorde House, Grenville Place,
Mill Hill, London, NW7 3SA.

Published in the USA by Monarch Books 2001.

Distributed by:
UK: STL, PO Box 300, Kingstown Broadway, Carlisle,
Cumbria CA3 0QS;
USA: Kregel Publications, PO Box 2607
Grand Rapids, Michigan 49501.

ISBN 1 85424 522 8 (UK)
ISBN 0 8254 6011 5 (USA)

**British Library Cataloguing Data**
A catalogue record for this book is available
from the British Library.

Book design and production for the publishers by
Bookprint Creative Services
P.O. Box 827, BN21 3YJ, England.
Printed in Great Britain.

# CONTENTS

# INTRODUCTION

Motherhood is a privilege and a joy. It can also be lonely at times and the routine a little boring. One of the highlights of the week may be getting out of the house with the baby or toddler and meeting with other young mums. It's a relief to share experiences, anxieties and frustrations with others in the same boat. Running such a group may seem an insignificant calling but it can be a life-saver to a lonely mother, and is a wonderful opportunity to serve the community.

## *Study time*

The studies provided in this book are to give the leaders some ideas which they can then put into their own words. They come in eleven sets of seven studies. Each set is on a different topic. The leader is free to choose to work through all seven of a set, or just two or three because, in most instances, each study stands on its own. There are suggested discussion points and simple visual aids which serve to keep the focus. If they would be helpful – use them, but be flexible. Some of the studies are particularly suitable for mothers but others are more general in nature. All carry a Christian message.

It is up to each leader to decide whether to include a short time of worship and a short prayer. If children are present, which they most likely will be, an action song for their benefit might be a good idea.

### The crèche option

Not all young mums are happy to put their children in a crèche – nor are the children happy to be left there. When the children stay with their mothers for the whole time group leaders often think that the presence of the children prohibits them having any kind of a study or sharing time with the parents. However, it is amazing how mothers soon develop the gift of doing two things at once, such as listen to someone speak and simultaneously watch a toddler at play, or feed their baby.

It may be a good idea to provide a crèche for the mums who would like a break from their children, and are happy to leave them. However, we must be sure that no expectation, either by word or look, is put on a young mum who is nervous of being separated from her child before she or the child is ready.

For this reason the studies in this book are short and should last no more than ten minutes, less if the children are particularly restless.

### Aims for group

The aim of such a group is to provide a place where parents can come and feel welcomed, accepted, encouraged, build relationships and experience the love of Christ through other members of the group. The Christian message has the greatest impact when it is put across, as Jesus did so often, through word and deed. The group may be made up entirely of Christians, in which case having a short study is no problem. But in many cases the group will consist of a mixture of those who attend the church and those whose only contact is the Mothers and

Toddlers (or Babies) group. For a mixed group it may not be wise to have confrontational evangelism, but to think more in terms of friendship evangelism. It may even be wise to make the ten-minute study optional. This may be the first time some members of the group have crossed the threshold of church premises, or mixed with Christians. It is worth making sure their encounter is as sweet as if they had met with Jesus for the first time. To have a short study in such a group is a bonus, but should not be the 'law of the Medes and Persians'. In other words, it is important for a leader to 'play it by ear'. How much or how little study is undertaken will vary with each group and even from week to week.

### Hints for leaders

There is an art in leading group Bible studies! Most importantly, be relaxed, be flexible and be friendly. Give the group permission to chip in with their ideas. Make sure the discussion points are put across in such a way as to provoke thought and don't give rise to 'Yes' or 'No' answers. When someone doesn't give a correct answer to a question, make sure you find something positive to say about the answer. 'Thank you, that's a very interesting point. Let's see if anyone else has a suggestion.' As far as possible use your own words, rather than reading the script straight from the book. Be sympathetic with any mum who is having a job restraining her toddler. A frown will put them off. Understanding will bring them back.

It's good to offer a cup of coffee and biscuits to the members, and sometimes even arrange a bread and cheese lunch for those who can stay. Food is a useful means of relaxing people and breaking down barriers. It's good to combine manna from heaven with a little manna from the supermarket!

But rest assured your labour will not be in vain. 'As the rain and the snow come down from heaven, and do not return to it without watering the earth and making it bud and flourish, so that it yields seed for the sower and bread for the eater, so is my word that goes out from my mouth: It will not return to me empty, but will accomplish what I desire and achieve the purpose for which I sent it' (Isaiah 55:10–11).

# CHAPTER ONE

# FAMILY MATTERS

Sons are a heritage from the Lord, children a reward from him. (Psalm 127:3)

# THEME – NURTURE

## *Materials:*

A potted plant, a bottle of plant food, some water and clippers.

## *Talk:*

(Explain about nurturing a potted plant.) Most of us have owned a potted plant which died from neglect of some sort. Plants need to be nurtured. They need to be carefully watered, fed, dead headed, and, now and again, pruned. (Demonstrate with your plant.)

Children also need nurturing. In this way they will grow and develop normally. If neglected they will become stunted and damaged.

## *Reading: Psalm 131:2, Isaiah 66:13*

The first verse refers to the contentment and tranquillity of a child who has just been fed. The next likens the comfort that Israel will receive from God, to the way a mother comforts her child. God created mothers, and in these verses acknowledges the incalculable part they play in their children's lives. Not only do their mothers give them birth, then care for them in those early months, but they continue to nurture, teach and encourage them throughout their childhood. When God was reassuring His people that He would never forget them, He asked them an unthinkable question: 'Can a mother forget the baby at her breast and have no compassion on the child she has borne?"(Isaiah 49:15). Though it is very unlikely, being human she may. But the majority of mothers naturally love their children.

Although at first it may seem that nurture is nothing but providing food, in fact it is much more than that. Children need emotional nurture as well as physical nurture, and they receive that from mother's presence. They need to be able to look into mother's eyes and see her love and concern reflected there. It has been said that mother's eyes are the beacon light of identity. Nurture involves eye contact and lots of cuddles, as well as food. The family therapist Virginia Satir has said that a child needs four hugs a day just for maintenance. So that child must need many more for growth. Later as the child matures he or she will also need to be nurtured spiritually and mentally. All this takes time, of course. And time is the one thing we are often short of. We live in a frenetic society and even though we may have a house full of labour-saving appliances, we still don't have enough time. It's tempting to place a baby in a swing chair to keep him quiet, or later, in front of the television, so that Mum can get on with something else. To an extent these things are a blessing, but not when they rob children of the most important person in their life. Someone has said that the greatest gift God gives your children is you!

### Discussion:

What are some practical ways in which we can nurture our children emotionally and spiritually?

## THEME – DISCIPLINE

**Materials:**

Flip chart or blackboard.

**Talk:**

(Tell the story of the island with precipitous sides.) Once upon a time there was an island with very steep sides. To keep themselves and their children safe the islanders built a fence all the way around the island. One day a boat sought refuge in their harbour and the islanders gave the boat crew hospitality for several weeks while they repaired the boat. Before the sailors left they told the islanders that they ought to take the fence down. 'You are all prisoners behind that fence,' they said. 'Think of the freedom and wonderful views you would enjoy if you took it down.' So the islanders took the fence down.

A year later the sailors returned to visit their friends. On arrival they found the terrified islanders huddled together, clutching their children, in the centre of the island. Rather than robbing them of their freedom, the fence had provided them with a secure environment within which they were free to live their lives. Removing it had robbed them of that freedom.

**Reading: Jude 21 (Living Bible)**

God's commandments are, for us, like a boundary fence. If we stay within the fence we are safe and blessed. If we stray outside we are likely to come to harm. They are given for our good and not to curtail our enjoyment of life, as some think!

God sets boundaries for us because He loves us. If we love our children then we must set appropriate boundaries for them too. To be any use boundaries need to be reasonable and not too rigid, otherwise our children can feel trapped and that stirs up rebellion. Once the boundaries have been made clear then children need to know the penalty for breaching them. But remember the punishment must always fit the crime. Today corporal punishment is not encouraged, but the principle behind the proverb: 'Spare the rod and spoil the child' (Proverbs 23:13) is still valid. Discipline is important so we have to think up appropriate punishments for our children when they are disobedient.

### *Discussion:*

Ask the group to share some practical ideas for disciplining children. Make a list using the flip chart.

Whatever the punishment, let's not forget the cuddle after the punishment is over. No child should ever feel he is loved less because he is naughty and has been punished. Whatever he does he is still your child. Jesus didn't leave Peter in misery, feeling an outcast for long after his denial. He gave him some special time and attention and in fact demonstrated His confidence in him by reinstating him. Our children need the same sort of treatment after being disciplined.

# THEME – COMMUNICATION

## Materials:

Mobile phone. (Call someone on the mobile phone and then explain how important communication is to us.)

## Talk:

Imagine how difficult it would be to live without a telephone. It is one of the most common ways of making contact with other people. Communication is vital and necessary for all of us, and people will overcome huge obstacles in order to communicate. Helen Keller, a well known writer and social reformer in the 19th century, was deaf, dumb and blind and lived in a totally blank world. Even so she found a way of communicating by making signs on her teacher's hand.

## Reading: John 1:1–5, 14

Our God is a communicating God. Down through the ages He has spoken to His people in many different ways. Finally Jesus came and was described as the Word made flesh. He was God's message of love to an estranged world. We have been made in the image of God, with the same ability and the same need to communicate. It is a powerful tool in our hands that may be used for good and evil. The old adage 'sticks and stones can break my bones but words can never hurt me', could not be further from the truth. Words can damage our hearts and affect us deeply.

(If there is time, open up the discussion for some sharing of experiences at this stage.)

If words have the power to hurt they also have the power to heal, especially in family life. It is said that the family that feels together heals together. The home should be a healing environment where the wounds received from the world outside can be soothed. But it only becomes a healing environment in so far as there is good communication within the family. Sadly, without meaning it parents have often added to their children's wounds by dishing out too much criticism and not enough encouragement. Studies have shown that in the average home, for every positive statement a child receives ten negative ones.[1]

### *Activity:*

Divide the group into pairs. If there is an uneven number the group leader will have to play, if not she can remain an onlooker. Tell the pairs that one is to be the speaker and the other the listener. Tell the speaker to share something about her last holiday, or a recent exciting family outing. The listener has to make a point of *not* listening. Look away, study her nails, yawn, etc. If there is time, change around and repeat the experiment. Then allow the group time to share how they felt.

### *Talk:*

Communication has two sides to it. There is the sharing and the listening. When our children share their fears and joys with us we have to listen, or the message they receive from us is that they are not valued and what they say has no importance to us. It is so easy to make a child feel loved and valued. Don't let's blow it!

## THEME – PRAYER

### *Materials:*

Flip chart or blackboard.

### *Talk:*

Bringing up a family can be a hazardous business. It is not easy to get it right, and we cannot always protect our children from sickness, difficulties, or pain. There will be times when we feel helpless and wish there was more we could do. A good habit to cultivate early on is prayer. Prayer *for* our children, and prayer *with* our children.

### *Reading: Philippians 4:6–7*

### *Discussion:*

Ask the group to state their hopes and fears for their families. Make a list of their contributions.

### *Talk:*

If these are the things we carry around inside us, then these are the 'everythings' we should be praying about. It is not always easy to share our hopes and fears with others, but we can share them with God; in fact He longs for us to do so.

So as we think about prayer and the family, the first thing to remember is to pray *for* them. We can do this wherever we are

– in the car, in the bath, while we cook. It isn't always easy to have a special time set aside to pray, especially when we have young children. Of course that would be the best thing, but we shouldn't feel guilty because it isn't always possible. God can hear us, even when we are pushing the pram to the shops.

The second thing to remember about prayer and the family is to pray *with* them.

The circumstances are not always right for a family prayer time. But if they are, remember to keep it short, make it relevant to the children by allowing them a share in what is prayed about, and don't be too rigid or formal. Sometimes there is not enough time for a long prayer, and a short prayer has to do. God understands and answers according to what's in our hearts, not how many words we use.

Then, of course, there is the prayer at bedtime. It's tempting to cut this short because we can hardly wait for that little bit of peace and quiet when the children are in bed. The Bible says: 'Train a child in the way he should go and when he is old he will not turn from it' (Proverbs 22:6). In the long term this habit of prayer will prove to be of value in our children's lives.

At first the prayer will be said over the baby in the crib, but as the child gets older he or she should become more involved. Young children need to be encouraged to thank God for the good things of the day, to pray about anything that has worried them, and to remember family and friends. Older children should be encouraged to talk to God about the sort of day they have had at school. It might be a good idea to keep a little book where the children can note down the things they have prayed about, and then tick them off as they see answers to those prayers.

Prayer for our children or with our children should never be a duty, only a privilege.

# THEME – TEACHING

*Materials:*

A table napkin.

*Activity:*

A napkin-folding demonstration.

1. Ask two people to participate. One person is to tell someone else, without actions, how to fold a napkin for a special dinner party. At the same time the other person has to try and follow the instructions.
2. Then ask another two people to do the same task, but this time using only actions and no words.

(Explain that of course it's easier to do the folding with both visual and verbal instruction.)

*Talk:*

Our children are born with an insatiable desire to acquire new skills. Providing toddlers are relatively secure they will naturally be on a daily journey of discovery. Automatically they will be absorbing what they see around them. Consciously or unconsciously, parents become models for their children's lives. Our homes are fast-track academies of learning.

So the question we need to ask ourselves is what are we teaching our children in the years of 'home' schooling? We model such things as patience, self-control, manners and faith. We demonstrate how to handle frustration, conflict and pressure. When you put behaviour together with words, our children are receiving powerful instruction.

From the beginning our children learn values and principles for living from us. All too soon the media becomes a significant teaching source and later peer pressure comes into play. Only then will we discover how firmly rooted the values we have tried to pass on to our children have become.

### *Reading: Deuteronomy 4:8–9*

Most importantly, we are responsible for teaching our children about God and worship. Again we teach it through our lives and our words. The Israelites were encouraged to pass on to their children God's laws as well as the stories about His wonderful deeds.

Are we passing on, through life and word, a testimony to the goodness of God?

*Materials:*

A list of the four different personalities for each person to consider.[2]

**Sanguine** – Fun loving, optimistic, humorous, forgetful, unpunctual, spontaneous, a talker.

**Choleric** – Organised, inflexible, sets goals, single minded, responsible, motivated, energetic, a leader.

**Melancholy** – Serious, a thinker, neat, talented, sincere, steadfast, high standards, perfectionist, can get depressed.

**Phlegmatic** – Relaxed, patient, sympathetic, avoids confrontation and conflict, easy going, pleasant, responds to situations rather than initiates, undisciplined, a follower.

*Activity:*

Give out the sheets of paper with your list on and let the group study them. Ask them to tick the one they identify with most closely.

*Talk:*

Most of us looked at that list and recognised our personality type quite easily. The list is like a marker which says, 'that's me'. We could even put ourselves into groups of those with similar personalities.

In the same way children need markers, especially with regard to their sexuality. The family therapist Robin Skynner says that a child needs two landmarks to get his bearing sexually and find out where he is and he needs them to be a certain distance apart.[3] The two markers are, of course, the parents – mum and dad!

Life is pressurised and time is scarce, especially for men. Often our children suffer the consequences. One-parent families are on the increase. Even so it is important that we encourage the father of our children, or a good father substitute, to relate to our children on a fairly regular basis. Perhaps if the natural father is not available a grandfather or uncle could become more involved.

There are many reasons why a child needs a father figure:

1.  First of all a father is there to interrupt the closeness which develops naturally between a mother and her baby, which would be unhealthy if it continued for too long. After that he provides the toddler with a landmark to differentiate between the sexes.
2.  Children also need to have encouragement from their fathers. The support children receive from a father, or a father substitute, seems to stimulate them to greater effort than that which they receive from a mother.
3.  As children enter their teens both sexes need to hear that masculine voice of affirmation. The teens are never a comfortable time for our children and they long to hear Dad's voice in particular, telling them they are O.K. And the affirmation should have nothing to do with achievement. God the Father was very affirming of Jesus even before He had started his public ministry. 'This is my beloved son in whom I am well pleased', were the words Jesus heard at his baptism.

Every child longs to hear words like that from their father.

*Reading: Psalm 127:3–5*

## THEME – FAIR PLAY

### Materials:

One cake big enough to feed the whole group, and a knife.

### Activity:

Tell the group that a cake has been provided for them to enjoy. Ask someone to cut it up. Let the group watch while she counts the heads and divides it into the correct number of pieces.

### Talk:

(Ask the person who divided the cake where she learned to share in such a fair manner.) Fairness and sharing are not things that come naturally. In fact selfishness comes more naturally to us. Many of the conflicts between children are about fair play and sharing. But at some point in our childhood most of us learned to share with others.

So how can we help our children to be generous and unselfish?

### Reading: Luke 10:25–28

The lawyer wanted to know how he could inherit eternal life. The answer Jesus gave him is one which, if put into practice, would also resolve many of the difficulties we have in family life.

If we want our children to learn to live happily with others, there are certain things we have to do:

1. We must love God and be consistently kind to others, because our children copy what they see in us, and will automatically follow suit. They won't buy into a way of life we talk about but don't live out in practice.
2. We must start building up their self-esteem if we want our children to love others. Jesus said that we were to love others *as* we love ourselves. It follows that if we don't love ourselves we aren't going to be able to love others. So we have to help our children come to a place of self-acceptance:
   - by helping them to communicate how they feel
   - by loving them unconditionally
   - by showing pride in the simple fact that they are our children
   - by encouraging them in the things they do well
   - by working with them to improve the things they find difficult.
3. We must share our love of God with our children and help them to love God with us. Involving them in our faith will make it more real to them.
4. Lastly, share our love of other people with our children and help them to love others with us. So if we have invited an elderly relative or friend to tea, instead of moaning about the visit in front of children, share the fact that the person is lonely and this will be a special treat for her. Help our children to take delight in giving someone else pleasure and involve them in entertaining the visitor.

Lastly, remember all small children find it difficult to share – it's an accomplishment they will learn given time and good assistance.

## CHAPTER TWO

# WHO AM I?

Understanding your identity in Christ is absolutely essential to your success at living the Christian life. No one can consistently behave in a way that is inconsistent with the way they perceive themselves. (Neil Anderson)

## THEME – THE IMPORTANCE OF IDENTITY

*Materials:*

Sufficient A4 paper for the whole group. Pins.

*Activity:*

Ask the group to write an answer to the question, 'Who Are you?', without using their name. Then pin the A4 paper with their answer to their fronts and circulate. Give as long as necessary for everyone to share with at least two or three other people.

*Talk:*

(First draw attention to what they have written on their paper. Most likely it will be concerned with activity, attachment, achievement, or appearance. Reassure the group that the way we tend to describe ourselves is perfectly normal.) However, these observations tend to be variable. Our work may change. Our friends and family move. We ourselves change in appearance and ability as we grow older. With any big change our identity feels threatened. (Perhaps give a personal example.) Yet a secure identity is crucial for the maintenance of emotional and mental health.

John Powell, a well-known writer on personal growth, says that the attitude each of us has toward the self is the most important of all our attitudes and that the attitude toward the self is always in play, always affecting our other attitudes, always colouring the way we see every part of reality.[4] Most of all, it affects our behaviour. Neil Anderson says that 'no person can behave in a way that is inconsistent with the way he perceives himself'.[5]

### Reading: Matthew 3:13–17

Wonderfully assuring words! Just for a moment try and remember whether you ever heard similar words of affirmation from your own father. (Leave some time for them to think.) If you did not hear such words, it doesn't mean that your father was not a good man or didn't love you – but just that most men do not realise how important such affirmation is to their children. These words from His Father came at the right time for Jesus because soon afterwards His identity was put under threat. He was led into the desert to be tempted by Satan, and the enemy cunningly prefaced two of those temptations with the question: '*If* you are the son of God . . .' '*If* you are the son of God . . .' But Jesus ignored the insinuation and the doubt challenging His identity. He had received that vital assurance from His Father and nothing could shake His security in who He really was.

It is important, especially in the uncertain age in which we live, to know our true identity. 'Who am I?' is not a question any Christian should need to ask. Whatever changes come our way the identity we have received from God cannot be shaken.

## THEME – AN UNSHAKABLE IDENTITY

*Materials:*

A bowl, towel and small bottle of fragrant oil.

*Activity:*

Ask for a volunteer to have her feet washed. Then ask another to wash that person's feet (or do it yourself). Finish by giving the feet a massage with oil.

*Reading: John 13:2–5*

*Talk:*

We have just watched one person wash and massage another's feet. In this day and age such a task may not be quite as menial as it once was. We have masseurs, chiropodists, and pedicurists today who will care for our feet. But in Jesus' day 'feet washing' was a job for the slaves of the household. After walking around the streets of Jerusalem or over the hills of Galilee, the disciples' feet would have been thick with dust and grime or worse. Upon their arrival at someone's house they would normally need to have their feet washed, unlike us today. On this occasion the Lord and his disciples were already sitting down, and the meal was being served, when Jesus got up from the table to do what should have been done already. Apparently no servant had come forward to wash the guests' feet, and none of the disciples had thought it was their place to do it.

A secure personal identity will affect the way we live our lives. So often we spend our time proving to others that we are people of value. We live with the equation that our value depends upon our performance and other people's opinion of us. Many of us live with a poor self-image and this either paralyses us so that we are afraid to attempt very much for fear of failure, or it galvanises us into actions which we hope will prove our personal worth to others, which we inwardly doubt.

Inside a 'pushy' person there is often a nobody trying to prove he is a 'somebody'. The security Jesus had in His identity meant that He had nothing to prove. He didn't have to strive to be a 'somebody'. It meant that Jesus was equally at home at the table of an important Pharisee as He was in the humble home of Mary and Martha, talking to a Samaritan woman of dubious reputation or touching an unclean leper. It meant that no menial task could diminish His sense of value.

In the verses that we read it says that Jesus *knew* certain things – that He had come from God and was returning to God. Then we find that important little word 'so'. 'So he got up from the meal took off his outer clothing, and wrapped a towel around his waist . . . and began to wash his disciples' feet. . .'

Jesus was so confident of His identity that He was free to do this necessary, though demeaning, task. Then He told His disciples that He had set an example for them to follow.

It is not easy to serve others when we are concerned about our self-image. Once we know who we are we can then relax in that knowledge because there is nothing left to prove.

## THEME – CHOSEN

*Materials:*

A picture of a family tree. A birth certificate. In advance, ask all, or several, members of the group to bring photos of themselves as babies.

*Activity:*

Pass round the photos for all to see. Show them the family tree and the birth certificate.

*Talk:*

The family tree shows us where someone came from – his or her ancestors. The birth certificate shows us who the parents were, and the photos show us how the baby looked. But none of these can tell us just how the parents felt about their baby. Were you a wanted child? Just think for a moment. (Give them time to think about it.)

Many people think that they were an accident, a mistake or an inconvenience. Even though the parents may have grown to love them, at the time of their conception they were unwelcome. Others for some reason have never felt special. Such people spend time trying to prove somehow that they have a right to exist, or to apologise in some way for their presence.

The late Henri Nouwen, who wrote many books on the spiritual life, seemed to understand the feelings so many carry within them. He wrote: 'As I look within as well as around myself, I am overwhelmed by the dark voices telling me, "You are nothing special, you are just another person among millions; your life is just one more mouth to feed, your needs just one more problem to solve."'

But he goes on to encourage us to stop listening to these voices. 'As long as we allow our parents, siblings, teachers, friends and lovers to determine whether we are chosen or not, we are caught in the net of a suffocating world that accepts or rejects us according to its own agenda.'

No, he says, 'Our preciousness, uniqueness and individuality are not given to us by those who meet us in clock-time – our brief chronological existence – but by the One who has chosen us with an everlasting love, a love that existed from all eternity and will last through all eternity.'

### Reading: 1 Peter 2:9

Again I quote from Henri Nouwen. 'From all eternity, long before you were born and became a part of history, you existed in God's heart. Long before your parents admired you or your friends acknowledged your gifts or your teachers, colleagues and employers encouraged you, you were already "chosen". The eyes of love had seen you as precious, as of infinite beauty and of eternal value.'[6]

Whatever the circumstances of our birth, we were chosen by Almighty God. You may have been a mistake or an inconvenience to your parents, but to God you were a planned and wanted child from all eternity.

## THEME – BELOVED

*Materials:*

Paper and pens, CD of 'The Father's Song' from the album of same name by Matt Redman.

*Activity:*

Ask the group to write down on paper what they think God feels when He looks at them. Then share what they have written with the group.

*Talk:*

In his book *The Singing God*, Sam Storms tells the story of a woman called Susan. Susan had had an unhappy life with a tyrant of a father whom she could never please. Consequently Susan could not believe that God really loved her. Nothing Sam said had any impact upon her, until he asked her the question 'What does God feel when He looks at you?' 'Pity,' Susan replied. 'Why?' asked Sam. 'Because I am pitiful and pathetic.' Sam tried to explain how much God loved her but to no avail. Then he asked her to read aloud a passage of Scripture:

The passage Sam chose was our reading from:

*Reading: Zephaniah 3:17*

'That's how God feels about you, Susan,' said Sam. 'He looks at you, He thinks of you, and He sings over you.' She was stunned. 'God sings? Over me?' After a few moments Susan

began to cry. 'Sam, are you sure?' she asked. Sam got her to read
the passage again. The tears returned; 'If only I could believe it
were true. I think then I could face almost anything. If only it
were true.'[7]

Well, it is true. In our search for identity we may turn anxiously
towards other people to tell us who we are, or we may fix on our
performance, or our appearance, to give us a sense of identity.
Am I what I do? Am I what other people think of me, am I what
I look like, am I what the culture dictates, am I who I relate to?
The search is over when we find our place in the heart of God.
Then we can say: 'I am loved by Almighty God therefore I am.'

### Reading: Colossians 3:12

We have to let the truth of our belovedness sink into our hearts
and penetrate our whole being. We need to live, day in and day
out, in a knowledge that goes far beyond our minds, but actually becomes 'who we are'.

### Suggestion:

Play 'The Father's Song' to the group.

## THEME – WORSHIPPERS

*Suggestion to leader:*

Borrow the video of 'Simon Birch' before the meeting and view it.

*Talk:*

Tell the group the story of 'Simon Birch'. This film concerns a very small boy who was born with a disability that kept him from growing normally. He is convinced that God has a purpose for his life and will use the way he looks to do something special. Simon is always asking people if they think God has a purpose for them, which seems to make them very uncomfortable. The pastor of the church doesn't like Simon asking these awkward questions. But Simon persists. The film ends with Simon finding the special purpose that God had for him.

*Discussion:*

Do you think God has a purpose for your life and if so, what is it? (Give the group time to think and then share what they think that might be.)

In most homes children have their specific weekly jobs. One might be allocated the dusting, another the task of hanging out the washing. But each member of the family is required to keep his or her room tidy – that's a general rule. In God's family it works the same. God has specific plans and general plans.

### Reading: Matthew 22:34–40

In this reading we find our primary calling, which is to love and worship God. In fact this is our first and most important entrustment. It is out of worship that we will find the specific tasks that God has set for us to do. When Jesus met the Samaritan woman at the well of Sychar, He told her that God was looking for worshippers who would worship Him in Spirit and Truth. God is looking for worshippers! This must become a part of our identity.

This call to worship is not an easy one, especially for busy mums. There is a cost in terms of time and effort. In the letter to the Hebrews we are admonished to 'continually offer to God a sacrifice of praise – the fruit of lips that confess His name' (Hebrews 13:15). A good habit would be to conduct 'divine service three times daily between the taps in the kitchen!' Or when you are driving along in your car, or vacuuming the carpet. God doesn't mind where or when we worship him, only that we do so.

## Theme – Heirs together with Christ

### Materials:

A 21st birthday card with a large silver key stuck to it. A last will and testament (or a copy of one).

### Activity:

Pass the will and the card around so that everyone can see what they are.

### Talk:

When your children come of age they are given their own key for the front door of the house, which means they have freedom of access. When you make your last will and testament you bequeath your worldly goods to people that you love and care about, usually your family. They become your heirs.

### Reading: Romans 8:15–17

God doesn't just call us His children and stop there. We are children who are always welcome in our Father's presence, and are inheritors of all His riches. Have you ever been given some information which has not sunk in, until you have really experienced it? For example, you may be told that the M25 (or a major road near you) is very busy on a Friday evening. You hear it but decide to make your journey using that route anyway. It is only when you are trapped in the rush hour traffic and at a standstill that the information sinks in to the extent that you will never forget it, and do everything possible to avoid making that same mistake again. We can all probably think of similar experiences. (If there is time, stop and let the group share some examples of this.)

It is only too easy to live knowing a truth in our heads, but not allowing it to make a difference to the way we act or feel at all. This Bible passage tells us that we are heirs together with Christ of the riches of Heaven. But many of us live as if this were not true.

(Tell briefly the story of the Prodigal Son, emphasising the older son's response to the homecoming celebration.)

A father had two sons. The younger went off with his inheritance into the far country but the older son stayed at home and worked on his father's estate. The young prodigal eventually came home and the father, delighted at his son's return, ordered a celebration. The party was under way when the older son came home from working in the fields. His reaction to the situation was one of anger: 'All these years I've been slaving for you and never disobeyed your orders. Yet you never gave me even a young goat so I could celebrate with my friends.' The sad young man saw himself as a slave and not a son. He viewed his father as a hard slave-driver, not as a loving parent. The father's response to his son was to speak the truth to him: 'You are always with me, and everything I have is yours.' We can almost see the father shaking his head in disbelief at his eldest son's attitude. Every moment of every day the older brother had had access to his father's presence. He was his father's heir and was free to enjoy every single thing the father owned. But none of this had sunk in. The love, mercy and grace of his father went unappreciated.

I wonder if we fully appreciate all that we have in Christ. I wonder if we enjoy the grace that is ours? Or do we live by lots of rules and regulations; seeing God as a hard task-master, ready to show His displeasure at the first sign of a mistake. I wonder if we have learned to celebrate the fact that we are not just His children but heirs together, with Jesus, of all the riches of heaven?

## THEME – THE FAMILY LIKENESS

### *Materials:*

Some magazines with pictures of clothes, articles on health and beauty. A lovely plant or bunch of flowers.

### *Discussion:*

What was the first thing you thought of when you awoke this morning? Or what has primarily been occupying your thoughts today? (Share around the group – don't force anyone who doesn't want to share.)

### *Talk:*

No one has difficulty thinking about what is immediate, or obvious. It may be family problems, finances, appearance, or health. One of the secrets of St Paul's life was that he disciplined himself not to limit his attention to everyday problems. They were just temporary issues. Instead, he learned to fix his thoughts on the unseen things that would be significant for all eternity. The everyday problems shout at us, demanding our attention, whereas what is unseen – the eternal things of God – are often silent, even though they are, in fact, more important.

For example, the media bombards us with advertisements telling us how to keep our bodies attractive, fashionable, thin, or healthy (hand around the magazines). This has a tendency to make us rather self-conscious, and even though we may not want to be preoccupied with how we look, we tend not to be able to help ourselves.

Of course God is not unmindful of our appearance. But Jesus told us not to worry about it – not to be anxious about how we look. He said that we should consider how our Heavenly Father provides for the birds and the lilies, who are more splendid than even King Solomon in all his glory. And it is true that as we look around at God's creation we are frequently amazed by His extravagant use of colours and shapes.

*Activity:*

Look at the flowers – notice the shapes and the colours.

God doesn't play down appearance. He just doesn't want us to be anxious about it and thinking about it all the time. But there is something about us that does concern God very much, and that is whether or not we are shaping up to be more like Jesus. Are we pleasant, loving and considerate of others? St Paul says that we are, or should be, the aroma of Christ to others.

*Reading: Romans 8:29*

God has actually planned for us to bear the family likeness. Whatever other changes may take place in us, the most important is whether or not we are changing to be more like Jesus. When clock-time is over and only eternity is left, the important factor will not be whether we are fat or thin, beautiful or plain, but whether people see Jesus in us. When we have lived with someone for a number of years we start talking and behaving like that person. So as we spend more time in the presence of Jesus we will find that, little by little, we are being transformed into His likeness.

You may be Mary, Jane, Anne, etc. (name a few of the people there). You may be a housewife, a mother, a breadwinner. But more importantly you are: a chosen and beloved child of Almighty God, an heir with Christ of all God's riches, a worshipper who is gradually becoming more like Jesus.

# CHAPTER THREE

# GLIMPSES OF THE KINGDOM OF GOD

'This is how you should pray: "Our Father in heaven, hallowed be your name, *your kingdom* come, your will be done on earth as it is in heaven."' (Matthew 6:9–10)

I will open my mouth in parables, I will utter things hidden from of old. (Psalm 78:2)

## THEME – THE GROWTH OF THE KINGDOM

*Materials:*

A collection of small seeds (apple seed, acorn etc.).

*Activity:*

Pass seeds around and let the group study and identify the seeds.

*Talk:*

Explain that all plants and trees start small – some very small indeed. But given the right conditions they are able to grow and benefit the world in some way.

*Reading: Matthew 13:31–32*

Jesus said that this is what the Kingdom of Heaven is like. It starts small and gradually grows bigger until it becomes something of worth and benefit to the world around.

Let's consider this for a moment! How did Christianity start? A young carpenter from a small village in Galilee was crucified like a common thief. His twelve terrified followers hid in an upper room in fear of the authorities. What an unpretentious start to a movement which would one day span the globe! Yet the incarnation of Jesus sliced history into two parts. The coming of Christ became the pivotal point of history. Just about every nation on earth must now be using BC and AD as the marker for their calendars. Christianity has spread around the world and is growing as never before. In places like Latin America and Africa prayer meetings frequently attract 50,000 people at one go! One person was buried, like a small seed, and from that death rose a great tree which has gathered millions of people into its shade.

Now think how it began in your own life. For most of us it began with something almost insignificant – a thought, a word, a need, an invitation, but gradually that small seed took root and began to grow.

(Ask one or two of the group to share how they came to faith.)

As the Kingdom of Heaven grows within a person it has the capacity to attract and give shelter to others.

(Give an example from a local Christian work of compassion, or use the following.)

A young twelve-year-old Albanian girl felt a call to become a nun. At the age of twenty-two she went to Calcutta to teach in a convent there. As she became aware of the desperate plight of the dying poor in that city a seed of compassion was sown in her heart. Eventually she began a work amongst them. A small seed gradually grew into a mission which today spans some of the world's worst slums. Mother Theresa is now dead but her work of compassion continues.

The Kingdom of Heaven starts small, but just like one of these seeds (point to the seeds you have brought with you) it has within it the power to grow and grow until it is a tree capable of producing good wholesome fruit in our hearts and in the world.

## THEME – THE VALUE OF THE KINGDOM

### Materials:

Some empty bottles of unlabelled medicines.

### Talk:

We have all read stories of families who have sacrificed a great deal in order to obtain treatment for a sick child. They may have had to sell up and move for a time to somewhere like the United States. Occasionally we read of recent discoveries which may keep us all alive for longer. Imagine if these bottles (show the bottles you have brought with you) contained an elixir that would keep you all young and beautiful forever. We would all want it. Anyone would make a great sacrifice for something that could achieve those results.

### Reading: Matthew 13:44–46

In this parable Jesus gave us an idea of the value of God's Kingdom. He said it is like a treasure hidden in a field which is so valuable that a man would sell everything he possessed to buy the field and own the treasure. What single thing would we sell all our possessions to acquire? (Ask for suggestions.)

One thing would be the cure for a terminal illness which had struck down a family member. Yet in a sense that is what the whole world is suffering from. It is as if we all have a genetic defect which will eventually kill us, and the only hope of life is Jesus. So the good news of the Kingdom is that there is a cure

for our terminal illness, which the Bible calls sin. The problem
with the word 'sin' is that it doesn't give us the sense of urgency
which we need. Most of us would admit that we have done, said
and thought wrong things, but nothing too drastic – nothing
that would deserve the sentence of death. But we overlook or
ignore God's holiness. It's like a burning fire. Nothing that is
not absolutely pure could endure in His presence. But besides
being holy He is totally just and totally loving. So to satisfy His
justice and His love He sent Jesus to pay the penalty for our sin
on the cross. Now when we repent and turn to Him we can
become as innocent as though we had done nothing wrong.
Because of Jesus we can be made absolutely pure, which is what
God in his holiness demands. This is why the Kingdom of
Heaven is like a treasure. Its value is incalculable.

But the other thing Jesus said in this parable is that the treasure
is a hidden one. There is nothing obvious about God's
Kingdom. It doesn't advertise itself in the way we are accus-
tomed to. If we went by the adverts on the television, everything
from cereal to holidays in the Caribbean are absolutely vital for
our happiness and good health. God's Kingdom doesn't boast
or draw attention to itself in so loud a fashion.

If God's Kingdom is hidden, how then do people find it?
Usually because they are searching for answers. Jesus said: 'Ask
and it will be given to you; seek and you will find; knock and
the door will be opened to you. For everyone who asks receives;
he who seeks finds; and to him who knocks, the door will be
opened' (Luke 11:9–10).

## THEME – THE CITIZENS OF THE KINGDOM

*Materials:*

Flip chart or blackboard.

*Activity:*

Ask everyone in the group to think about some of the main characteristics of small children. Then discuss the different adjectives and make a list. (Words such as: dependent, innocent, spontaneous, trusting, open, frank.)

*Reading: Mark 10:13–15*

*Talk:*

People brought their children to Jesus because they wanted Him to bless them. Perhaps they did so because He was gaining a reputation as a rabbi in the region and they wanted to be able to boast: 'My child was blessed by Rabbi Jesus.' Or perhaps they were a little superstitious and thought Jesus was some sort of 'guru' with supernatural powers. Some may have seen something different, even holy, about Jesus and just wanted their children to be near Him.

Jesus did not seem to be too concerned with their motives – why they had come. His main concern was that the disciples had tried to turn them away. He was probably indignant for several reasons. One, because He didn't like His disciples presuming He would have no time for little children. They had decided what

Jesus liked and disliked without apparently asking Him or even giving much thought to it.

It is strange that though they were constantly with Jesus they could misread Him so easily. Their attitude towards Jesus was most likely one born from experience of other religious leaders who liked to be treated with special reverence and honour and would have found the presence of little children tiresome. The disciples may have presumed Jesus would be like that too.

We do the same so often. Don't we decide what God is like based on some preconceived idea we have? How many of us project the image of our own fathers on to God, expecting Him to be distant, abusive, kindly, weak, absent, silent – whatever our own fathers may have been like. We then wonder why we have problems relating to God as our Heavenly Father. Just like the disciples, we can get it wrong if we don't stop and find out the truth.

But He was also pained because they had their priorities wrong. It seems Jesus had had a long walk that day and crowds of people had come to hear him teach. The disciples knew He would be tired and wanted to protect Him from unnecessary hassle by insignificant little children. But children were as much a priority with Jesus as any adult – maybe even more so because in their innocence they were so open to believing the message. As far as Jesus was concerned only people with the attitude of little children would inherit the Kingdom of Heaven. God's Kingdom doesn't have room for independent, insincere, suspicious, self-centred people. The ambience of the Kingdom is completely different. It is one of trust, dependence and sincerity.

## THEME – THE PRINCIPLES OF THE KINGDOM

### *Materials:*

Enough small chocolate eggs for the whole group, including any children who might be present. Diplomas, cups, or rosettes for different achievements. A recording of the hymn, 'Amazing Grace'.

### *Talk:*

(Explain that when we have worked hard, or a member of the family has, we expect a reward.) A person who has been successful in passing an exam, or winning a race, should get something to prove his success. (Show the group the diplomas, cups, or rosettes.)

It is normal in most schools to have a prize-giving ceremony at the end of the year and we all hope that one of our children will get a mention. When the report card arrives we open it anxiously to see how our child has been marked and what position he or she has gained in the class. In our world children and adults are rewarded according to results. It is accepted as a just system.

### *Activity:*

Now let's play a game! (Encourage everyone, including any children, to search for three chocolate eggs which you have previously hidden. When they are found, congratulate the winners and tell them they can keep the eggs, but then bring out the rest of the eggs and give one to each person who went on the search.)

### Talk:

Now that's not exactly fair is it? Surely only the ones who found the eggs should be especially rewarded. In our world that's very often how it works, but things are different in God's world.

### Reading: Matthew 20:1–16

Here we have another glimpse into what God's Kingdom is like. If this sort of employment strategy were to be used in this country today our economy would soon collapse. Certainly our trade unions would be up in arms. But God's Kingdom is run on very different principles.

In God's house if you look for eggs, whether or not you succeed in finding one you would be rewarded for trying, because God loves us like a father loves his children and in His book the reward is not for success but for joining in and being a part of the game.

The men in Jesus' story had families to feed. Whether they had worked all day or for one hour, their needs were the same and their effort to find work was the same. Generosity and mercy are features of God's Kingdom. It is also a Kingdom run on grace not fairness, at least not our notion of fairness. For example, the thief on the cross beside the dying Jesus went to be with Him in Paradise even though he had done nothing to deserve it. All he had done was to ask Jesus to remember him when He came into His Kingdom. He received the same reward as St Paul, who preached the Kingdom all over the world and suffered many hardships in the process. It may not seem fair but in fact entrance to the Kingdom is never the reward for hard

work. Entrance to the Kingdom comes through trusting Jesus, whether it is at the beginning of a long life or on one's death-bed. Our God is a God of generosity, mercy and grace.
(Play the hymn 'Amazing Grace'.)

## Theme – The great banquet

**Materials:**

A white sheet.

**Talk:**

What would you do if it was your child's birthday and none of the children you had invited to his party could come? (Give the group time to make some suggestions.) One of the solutions would be to invite a different set of children, ones you would not normally have invited. For example, you could invite a family who had recently arrived in the area and knew very few people.

**Reading: Matthew 22:1–14**

The meaning of this parable is that the King, Almighty God, is throwing a party for His beloved son, Jesus. Those who were invited treated the invitation with contempt so the King opened the party up to anyone who would come. The invitation to the banquet went out far and wide. The surprising aspect of this Kingdom banquet was the number of mundane excuses given and that relatively few responded positively to the invitation. 'Many are invited, but few are chosen.' However, the ones who did respond became the 'chosen' ones: rather like the outsiders who may have been invited to your child's party. They would have been the chosen ones simply because they responded to the invitation. Certainly you would not treat them as second best. You would want them to feel like special guests. So when we respond to God's invitation we get a 'chosen' label to wear.

The story is full of surprises. What about the man who was thrown out because he was not wearing a wedding garment? At first glance this bit of the story seems to be rather harsh and out of keeping with God's mercy. Surely it is not fair to be penalised for being incorrectly dressed? Perhaps the poor man couldn't afford anything better. Imagine if your party had been a swimming party and one of the children had forgotten his swimsuit. You would probably provide him with a costume so that he wouldn't feel left out of the celebration.

It seems that the King in Jesus' story was incredibly generous and did not want anyone to feel embarrassed or out of place, so he provided a special wedding garment for each guest. The man who refused the garment most likely thought he was fit to come into the presence of the King and His son just as he was. This story underlines a very important Kingdom principle. God is a Holy God and no one can come into His presence relying on his/her own goodness. Not even our 'best' is good enough before the holiness of God. The prophet Isaiah reminded us that all our righteous acts are like filthy rags (Isaiah 64:6). We are all desperately in need of God's generous offer of a wedding garment. Imagine standing in God's presence with every shameful act we have ever committed plain for all to see. It would be unbearable. But God is a merciful God and has provided us with a garment of righteousness, so that we are covered and can stand before Him without shame. (Demonstrate with the sheet.)

St John saw this when he had that amazing vision on the Isle of Patmos. 'After this I looked and there before me was a great multitude that no one could count, from every nation, tribe, people and language, standing before the throne and in front of the Lamb. They were wearing white robes and were holding palm branches in their hands' (Revelation 7:9–10).

## THEME – THE DELAY OF THE KINGDOM

*Materials:*

An out of date passport, a wallet with just a few £10 notes.

*Talk:*

(Tell the following story.) A young girl meets a young man at a party and falls instantly in love! The only problem is that the young man comes from the United States and is hitching around the world. He has no job and no money. For a month they see each other every day. At the end of that time they promise each other that they will spend the future together. He says that he will go straight back home, find a job, save some money, get somewhere to live and then he will come back for her. Meanwhile she is to save every penny she can to buy her ticket to the USA.

They part company amid sad farewells and promises to stay faithful until they meet again. The young girl starts saving her money. Every week she puts aside £20. She makes sure her passport is up to date and buys a large suitcase. The weeks go by, and she hears nothing. The months pass and still nothing. Gradually her memory of him begins to fade and the enthusiasm for saving begins to wane. In fact she starts to use the money already saved to buy a few treats to alleviate her sad feelings. She begins to go out more and the money gradually disappears. Then one day there is a knock at the door and there he is – ready to claim his bride! She is shocked, and embarrassed.

She has no ticket and no money to buy one, and what's more her passport is now out of date. (Indicate with the out of date passport and the few £10 notes.)

### Reading: Matthew 25:1–13

Many of Jesus' parables about the Kingdom of Heaven are to do with the delay between His first coming and His second. The first was when He proclaimed God's Kingdom and established it in the hearts of His followers. The second coming will be when the Kingdom comes in its fullness and glory. Jesus knew the delay between the two would be difficult for many of us, so He used everyday examples to give us some idea of what to expect. In this one He illustrates it by pointing out the time between a betrothal and the actual wedding.

In one sense the first coming of Jesus was like a betrothal of marriage, an engagement. It was a promise of a relationship which would have its fulfilment when He returned for His bride, the church. His first coming was a taster of what was to come. The problem for those first disciples was that they felt sure that Jesus' return would be immediate. As the years have gone by we have all become a little like these foolish virgins or the girl in the story. We have stopped anticipating His return, and have become slack. This is a story warning us that although we cannot know the day or the hour of Jesus' return, we have to live as if it were going to be today.

### Discussion:

What sort of things can we do to stop ourselves from becoming slack?

## THEME – THE ECONOMICS OF THE KINGDOM

*Materials:*

A used football and a new one.

*Discussion:*

Imagine giving two new balls to two brothers at Christmas. Michael immediately started using his. Richard hasn't bothered. Which of these boys would you send to football coaching and why?

(Obviously Michael, because he has been using his gift until it is almost worn out, but Richard hasn't even bothered to play with his.)

*Reading: Matthew 25:14–30*

The talents that the man gave to his servants were pieces of money, but we could interpret the talents as something we are good at – a gift we have. In the story two of the servants put their talents to good use, but the last one buried his, fearing his master would be angry with him if he lost it. His excuse was that he knew his master was a hard man – he presumed that he knew what his master was like. Probably he had seen other landowners who were hard and unfair, and he expected his boss to be exactly the same.

It is only too easy for us to make the same mistake with God. We attribute to God the human characteristics which we have encountered in other authority figures we have known or heard of. By falling into that trap the servant missed the opportunity of using his talent for the benefit of his master's estate. We have to be on our guard lest we fall into the same trap and miss out, not just on using what God has given us, but also on enjoying a fulfilling relationship with God Himself.

In this parable Jesus was once more drawing our attention to the delay between His going and coming back again. But this time He was encouraging his disciples, not just to be ready for His coming, but to make good use of the time in between. A writer called Philip Yancey has said that the people of God are not merely to mark time, waiting for God to step in and set to right all the wrong. Rather, they are to model the new heaven and new earth, and by so doing awaken longings for what God will someday bring to pass.[8]

We are all different. We have different personalities and different gifts. How can we make good use of our gifts? How can we be models of the new heaven and the new earth – God's coming Kingdom? Let's think about God's Kingdom for a while. What do we know about it? (Give the group some time to share what they think.) It's a Kingdom of mercy, love, forgiveness, peace and joy. How can we use our talents, which are what we have as well as who we are, to share the Kingdom with others? (Give the group time to share.)

It is interesting that Jesus says the more we use our gifts the more we will have. In our illustration Michael used his football and so he was sent to football classes to increase his ability. As we use what we have for God He increases the little so that we have more. 'For everyone who has will be given more and he will have an abundance.'

# CHAPTER FOUR

# LESSONS FROM SEVEN WOMEN

Where the battle is the hottest in the battlefields of life
You will find the Christian soldier represented by his
  wife! – Unknown

## Theme – Miriam

### *Materials:*

£2 coin.

### *Talk:*

Today we want to look at a woman in the Bible called Miriam. She was the older sister of Moses, who led the people of Israel out of their enslavement in Egypt. It was Miriam who watched over her baby brother when he was hidden among the bulrushes to save him from being murdered by the Egyptians. Though just a young girl at the time, she showed amazing initiative, as well as sensitivity to the baby's needs. Pharaoh's daughter came down to bathe, heard Moses crying, opened the basket and felt sorry for him. Straightaway Miriam asked her if she should go and find a Hebrew woman to nurse the baby. Then she ingeniously fetched her own mother. So Moses' mother looked after him and was paid by Pharaoh's daughter for doing so.

### *Reading: Exodus 15:20–21*

Eighty years passed before Moses eventually led the people out of Egypt. It was an amazing deliverance and was celebrated by a song of praise to God in which Miriam, sensitive to the moment, took the initiative and led the women in singing and dancing. We know that she also had a gift of prophecy, which indicates a sensitivity to God. But there was a downside to this particular characteristic.

### Reading: Numbers 12:1–2

Miriam and Aaron began to criticise Moses, God's chosen leader. They had come to resent his Cushite wife and were jealous of his favoured position with God and the people. Miriam most likely thought that because she was older than Moses she deserved more recognition than she was receiving.

Miriam is a little like this coin. (Show the coin.) It is a valuable coin with two sides to it. Miriam was a woman of amazing gifts. She was very sensitive both to other people and to God. But she was also sensitive to perceived injustice, especially when it affected her. Most of us, like Miriam, tend to have an up and a down side to our character. Often our strengths can also be our weakness.

Think for a moment of someone who is very organised, tidy and punctual. These are excellent qualities, which mean they get more work done than others. But the down side is that they can be irritated by mess and impatient with others who are slower and less well organised than themselves. Their good qualities then become their enemy. (Illustrate, if possible, from one's own life.)

### Discussion:

Encourage the group to discuss times when they have experienced this phenomenon in their own lives.

It's good to face up to the down side in our own characters, because once we recognise it we are in a position, with God's help, to do something about it.

## THEME – DEBORAH

*Materials:*

Blackboard, flip chart or overhead projector.

*Discussion:*

Ask the group to list the distinctive characteristics of men and women and write them on the board.

*Talk:*

In God's sight men and women are equal. But we have to face the fact that we are not the same and never will be. We are equal but different and it's good to celebrate our differences sometimes.

*Reading: Judges 4:4–6*

Following five male judges Deborah took over as leader of Israel. She was a wife and probably the mother of a family. She was a multi-gifted woman – as many are! She had the wisdom to settle disputes. She listened to God. She was a songwriter, and the head of the army depended on her for support.

Deborah proved to be an amazing woman of God and a great leader. But it is interesting to note that the title she gave herself, and the one by which she has been known down through the ages, is one which acknowledged her womanhood and her major gifting as a matriarch 'Deborah, a mother in Israel'. This woman undertook work that previously only men had done, but she did it with the touch and gifting of a woman. There is no denial here of her femininity; only a celebration of the special gifts, as a woman and mother, that she was able to bring to the job of leading a nation. Let us never denigrate the job of motherhood.

(Give some examples of mothers of famous men.)

It has been said that the hand that rocks the cradle rules the world. For example, Abraham Lincoln wrote a poem entitled: 'My Angel Mother':

All that I am, all that I hope to be
I owe my angel mother;
My hand she guided as I learned to write,
My feet she guided in the ways of right,
My hopes she cherished, like a flame of light,
God bless her soul, God bless her memory,
Nancy, my angel mother.

St Augustine of Hippo was known as 'the son of the tears of Monica' (his mother).

Then there was John Wesley, who wrote that his mother was the source from which he derived the guiding principles of his life.

### Discussion:

What do you think is the most significant way a mother can influence her children so that they will reach their full potential in life?

## THEME – RUTH AND NAOMI

*Materials:*

Three pieces of cord or rope.

*Talk:*

God did not create us to be alone. In fact, when He made the human race He said that it was not good for us to be alone. Friendship can be a wonderful gift to us. Life can be very lonely without true friends with whom we can share experiences. A marriage based on friendship is likely to be a lasting one.

However, friendship can go wrong. Most of us will have experienced a good relationship that has broken down for such reasons as jealousy, over-dependence, misunderstanding, or betrayal. So if friendship is something God intended, how can we enjoy it without these things creeping in and spoiling a relationship which was meant to benefit us?

(Introduce the story of Ruth.) Because of a famine in Israel a man and his wife went to live in the country of Moab. While there the man died, leaving his wife Naomi and two sons who married two Moabite women, Ruth and Orpah. Then the sons also died, and Naomi was left with her daughters-in-law. Hearing that the famine in Israel was over she decided to return to her own country. She told the two girls to go back to their mothers' homes, where she hoped they would both find husbands. But neither of them wanted to leave Naomi. They wept and begged to be allowed to go with her. Finally she persuaded Orpah to leave but Ruth remained adamant that she would stay with her mother-in-law.

### Reading: Ruth 1:15–18

So Ruth travelled to Bethlehem with Naomi. Once settled, Ruth went out to work in the fields of Boaz, a distant relative of Naomi. The story has a wonderfully happy ending with Ruth marrying Boaz and giving birth to a son called Obed, who was the grandfather of King David and therefore a direct ancestor of Jesus.

The women around Naomi praised God for the little boy, and especially for Ruth, whose love for Naomi had proved 'better to her than seven sons'. It is interesting to note that the name Ruth in Hebrew sounds very similar to the word for friendship.

The story of Ruth and Naomi is an illustration of a friendship which survived very hard times and some radically changed circumstances. Why was the relationship of the two women so blessed?

(Ask for suggestions – then show the three pieces of cord and wind them together. Demonstrate the strength of the three as opposed to the one on its own.)

Ecclesiastes 4:12 says that a cord of three strands is not quickly broken.

The secret of Ruth and Naomi's relationship was the added dimension – their faith in God. It was this that made all the difference.

## THEME – THE WOMAN AT THE WELL

*Materials:*

A pair of dark glasses and a happy mask on a stick. (This can be home-made.)

*Talk:*

Shame is a powerful emotion. It was probably the first bad feeling Adam and Eve experienced. After they disobeyed God the eyes of both of them were opened and they realised that they were naked; so they sewed fig leaves together and made coverings for themselves. Then when they heard God coming they hid themselves.

This a normal response to shame. We hope that others will not see our shame so we try to hide it in some way. We cover it up by pretending that we are fine and nothing is wrong (hide your face behind the mask). Or we literally hide ourselves, sometimes by withdrawing from others, or even hiding behind dark glasses (put the glasses on). The eyes are the windows of the soul, and we fear people will see what we are like if they can look directly into our eyes.

People suffer from shame for various reasons. They may have been humiliated by another person in a very public way, or they may have done something of which they are ashamed and they suspect, or fear, that other people know or will find out.

*Reading: John 4:4–7, 28–29, 39–42*

(Briefly explain the story of the Samaritan woman.) Jesus was passing through Samaria and felt weary so He rested by a well while His disciples went into the town to buy bread. Whilst He was waiting at the well a solitary woman came to fetch water. It was unusual both for a woman to come on her own, and for her to come in the heat of the day. The woman and Jesus had an amazing conversation about 'living water'. He then told her to go and get her husband, but she explained that she had no husband. 'You are right,' He said, 'when you say you have no husband. The fact is, you have had five husbands, and the man you now have is not your husband. What you have just said is quite true.' This was obviously the reason for her lonely trek in the midday sun to fetch water. She was ashamed of her lifestyle and withdrew from the company of other women. But when Jesus showed her that He knew all about her, she completely forgot her shame and ran back to the town to tell everyone about Him. Because of her testimony many went out to see Jesus and became believers.

In this story we see the 'expulsive power of a greater affection' (Thomas Chalmers). Until she had met Jesus her shame was foremost in her mind. It controlled her life. But after her conversation with Him she forgot it. She went towards people, not away from them. Jesus is the one who can heal the pain of being shamed, and cleanse us from the shame of past misdeeds.

## THEME – MARY THE MOTHER OF JESUS

### Materials:

An item of baby clothing, a child's school textbook, and a piece of office equipment.

### Discussion:

(Have a short discussion on what the group thinks God's will is for them at this time in their lives.)

### Talk:

God has an entrustment for each of us. However, at different times in our lives the entrustment may change. At this moment our major entrustment is probably looking after a family (show piece of baby clothing and a child's textbook). But that entrustment will change as time goes by and another will emerge. It might be back in secular employment (show piece of office equipment), or looking after an elderly relative, being hospitable to lonely people, or even leading a Mums and Toddlers' meeting. When we are in the middle of one stage of our lives it's easy to become discontent and feel that our particular entrustment is boring and not very important. Then we may quickly become depressed and fail to enjoy the good things today offers. Another trap we can fall into is trying to cling to an entrustment after it has finished.

### Reading: Luke 1:26–38, Mark 3:21, 31–35

Mary is a wonderful example of how to embrace the will of God. She was asked to do perhaps the most difficult thing any

77

young teenager of her day could be asked to do. She was asked to bear a child, without being married and without knowing how the man she was engaged to would react. If he had followed social custom he would have had to expose her to public disgrace. This would have resulted in rejection from society. In the circumstances her response to God was amazing. She never once complained, but humbly accepted God's will. Jesus' subsequent birth was accompanied by many signs and wonders. Mary just stored them in her heart and got on with nurturing Jesus.

Jesus grew to manhood and embarked on His public ministry. His popularity was growing and crowds gathered wherever He went – to the extent that He often couldn't even sit down to eat. When His family, including His mother, heard about this they tried to rescue Him.

Mary found it hard to lay down the entrustment of looking after Jesus, even though He was clearly a grown man capable of taking responsibility for His own life and making His own decisions. She still wanted to interfere in His life.

God has an entrustment for each of us which may change at different times in our lives. It is important we embrace His will and enjoy it to the full, and then when it's over move on to the next phase of our lives.

## THEME – THE WOMAN WHO TOUCHED JESUS' CLOAK

*Materials:*

One chair.

*Talk:*

Few of us will put our trust in people, machines, or even a commodity that has not been thoroughly tested and recommended to us. We like to be sure that it will work and not harm us, or our family. We put our money in a bank with a good reputation. We only leave our children with someone we know to be responsible. We would be unlikely to cross a ravine on an untested suspension bridge. But when it comes to trusting God we have to exercise faith. Faith is a decision to trust God even though we can't see Him, feel Him, or touch Him. We don't have any absolute proof of His existence, nor if He exists whether or not He will hear us and respond to our prayers. We decide to trust Him for a variety of reasons. It makes sense that He exists, even if we can't see Him. It is not reasonable to believe that the world came into existence by accident and that there is no mastermind behind creation. We also trust Him because we have the testimony of millions of people through the ages who have found Him trustworthy. Also we have had some personal experience of His presence in our lives.

Place the chair in front of the group and tell them you cannot see all the legs. In fact you can probably only see two, perhaps three, from any given angle. But your experience of chairs,

79

other people's testimony, and logic tells you that there is a fourth leg hidden from view. So despite the risk you are willing to trust your weight to the chair. (Sit on the chair.) That's faith.

### Reading: Luke 8:43–48

This sick woman took a big risk. She was ceremonially unclean and should not have been mixing with people, let alone touching someone. If she had been spotted in the crowd there would have been a big hue and cry. She took a risk in touching Jesus' cloak. No one had been healed that way before. She must have been so desperate that her need overcame her doubt. Faith and doubt go hand in hand. If there was no doubt there would be no need for faith. But however small the faith is, it is the best conductor for healing. Jesus immediately felt that power had gone from Him and knew someone with faith had touched Him. The woman was healed at once. For the woman's own good Jesus made her admit it. He then commended her for her faith and told her to go in peace.

We should never worry if we sometimes suffer from doubts. FAITH is spelt R I S K, because faith always has an element of doubt to it.

## Theme – Mary and Martha

### *Materials:*

Flip chart or blackboard already prepared with a list of the following activities: making beds, cooking supper, shopping, reading Bible, fitness class, watching TV news, visiting a sick neighbour, cleaning silver, dusting, prayer, ringing a close relative.

### *Discussion:*

The group members have a very busy day coming up and on top of that their husband has invited friends over for supper. So they need to prioritise their activities. Ask them to say which of three activities they would place at the top of their list. (Each person will probably have a different order of priorities.)

### *Talk:*

Our practices are evidence of those things we value. Out of our values we set priorities, which we then put into action. For example, if we really value our health and like to be in good shape, then we prioritise the fitness class, and organise our day so that we have the time to attend. However, sometimes we may claim to value something while our practices show that in fact we don't really value it at all because we never put any time, money or energy into it. Some people might say they value their extended family, but they rarely ring them or visit them. If we truly valued them we would make time for them in our diary.

## Reading: Luke 10:38–42

Jesus often spent time in Bethany at the home of Mary, Martha and Lazarus. On this occasion the two sisters had a difference of opinion. Martha spent her time in the kitchen preparing the meal while Mary sat at the feet of Jesus and listened to His teaching. Not surprisingly Martha was fed up with Mary. She felt it was not fair that she should have been doing all the work, while Mary, in her view, did nothing. So she complained to Jesus.

Imagine yourself in Martha's place. How would you have felt? Probably annoyed at the apparent unfairness, as she was. Very surprisingly Jesus took Mary's side and rebuked Martha for having mistaken priorities in her life.

Mary and Martha obviously had a different set of values. Martha's were to do with being a good hostess. She wanted to provide well for everyone; perhaps that was important to her sense of self-esteem. Mary, on the other hand, loved being near Jesus and spending time listening to Him. It came high on her list of priorities. Food, and what people thought of her, came lower down. Jesus commended her for choosing the best part, which should not be taken over by something which could wait and was less important.

Martin Luther, the great reformer, is quoted as saying that he was so busy he found he could not do with less than four hours in the presence of God! Perhaps we need to re-think some of our priorities!

# CHAPTER FIVE

# KINGDOM CHARACTER

Having nothing, and yet possessing everything.
(2 Corinthians 6:10)

## THEME – A PARADIGM SHIFT

### *Materials:*

A picture of the Old Hag/Beautiful Young Girl. A recording of Frank Sinatra singing 'I Did It My Way', or failing that a copy of the words.

### *Talk:*

Jesus had only three years to teach His disciples about the Kingdom they would be left to represent. Most of them were ordinary, uneducated fishermen from a very rural part of Israel. The city people in Jerusalem would have called them 'country bumpkins'. Jesus' teaching, summarised in the Sermon on the Mount, provided the disciples with a foundation for life. His revolutionary Kingdom values and practices challenged the disciples, who had already formed their own ideas on how to run their lives and behave towards others and God. Just as we have.

### *Discussion:*

Let's just stop and think for a moment about our philosophy of life. What do we say to ourselves when in difficulties? (Give the group time to think and then share.)

We tend to say things like: 'I just have to cope.' 'Oh, Mum will help out!' 'No one is around when I need them.' 'It's not fair' (and look around for someone to blame!), or 'I can manage on my own.' Independence is one of the most common

responses in our western world where individualism is highly valued.

(Play 'I Did It My Way', or read the words)

According to J.B. Phillips, the world says:

> Happy are the 'pushers' for they get on in the world.
> Happy are the hard-boiled: for they never let life hurt them.
> Happy are they who complain: for they get their own way in the end.
> Happy are the blasé: for they never worry over their sins.
> Happy are the slave-drivers: for they get results.
> Happy are the knowledgeable men of the world: for they know their way around.
> Happy are the trouble-makers: for they make people take notice of them[9].

### Reading: Matthew 5:1–12

We often need to have our philosophy of life challenged. We need a paradigm shift.

### Activity:

Hand out copies of the Old Hag/Beautiful Young Girl. Ask the group what they see. Most will see the Old Hag first. Ask them to look for the Beautiful Young Girl. It is the same picture but a different way of seeing it.

### Talk:

Most of the disciples were independent, practical men. Jesus challenged all their preconceptions in this sermon. What Jesus was doing was turning their world view upside down. They received a paradigm shift. But it is a sermon for all time. It has a relevant challenge to the self-sufficient, self-reliant culture in which we live today.

## THEME – WEAKNESS AND BROKENNESS

*Reading: Matthew 5:1–4*

*Talk:*

'Blessed are the poor in spirit.' The disciples must have gasped when Jesus said this. What on earth did He mean? Jesus was talking about people who were aware of the spiritual poverty of their own souls, who knew they could do nothing to earn their salvation and that in reality they were totally dependent on God for mercy.

Jesus said these people are to be envied because theirs is the Kingdom of Heaven. Eternal life is a gift of God. This grace is on offer to everyone, but only beggars receive it – they are the ones who know they want it and can't pay for it.

The secular world mocks the Christian for needing a crutch. Well, it's the truth. The Christian has learned that he cannot live in independence. Dependence opens the gates of Heaven. Dependence is fundamental to life in God's Kingdom. People who realise they are totally dependent on God, Jesus said, are to be envied because 'theirs is the Kingdom of Heaven'.

Then when Jesus said: 'Blessed are those who mourn', another ripple of amazement must have gone around the crowd. How on earth could a person who is mourning be blessed? It didn't make sense. In fact it seemed a contradiction in terms.

But is it so contradictory? Can you remember the experience of waking up crying from a bad dream and being gathered up into the secure arms of your mother? If you can you will recollect what a relief and comfort it was. It was almost worth having the nightmare to experience the joy of being so comforted! Similarly, people who have woken up to the fact that they are sinners have a sense of guilt and grief. But once they realise that God's forgiveness is available their mourning is turned to joy and they are comforted.

However, our sin is not the only cause of mourning. We live in a world where hurt is inevitable and no one is exempt from suffering. Most of life's traumas are to do with loss – loss of love and friendship, loss of security, loss of self-worth, loss of work, etc. When a person can grieve properly and be comforted at the time of the trauma, the hurt gets healed. But if, as often happens, one suppresses the grief, then there is no healing and often a feeling of insecurity or low self-esteem remains. Such a person may suffer a lifetime of problems unless they find some help. Whether our pain is due to a present or past happening, the wonderful news is that Jesus loves to comfort those who grieve. King David said: 'The Lord is close to the broken-hearted and saves those who are crushed in spirit'(Psalm 34:18).

# THEME – HUMILITY

## Materials:

Find a variety of adverts in the Appointments section of the newspaper. Enlarge and highlight the words which describe the characteristics the secular world demands. Stick the adverts on a board.

## Talk:

The secular world is looking for men and women who are ambitious and have a hunger for success. The Rat Racers, who are willing to sacrifice their friends and family on the altar of success, are too often the ones admired and envied. To a degree we are all influenced by the prevailing attitudes around us. It is rather like breathing in polluted air. Everyone is affected by pollution, though they may not be guilty of causing it themselves. So, if we are honest, when we meet people who have reached the top by their own efforts, we are often slightly impressed and maybe even a little envious.

## Reading: Matthew 5:5

With these words Jesus turns our values upside down. In most people's eyes a meek person is to be despised, never admired, only pitied because meekness comes across as weakness.

(Briefly tell the story of Moses.) The story of Moses helps us to understand what Jesus meant. Moses was a Jew brought up in a palace as the adopted son of an Egyptian princess. Though he was treated like a prince and was waited on hand and foot, he didn't forget his own people. On one occasion he impulsively and arrogantly tried to rescue a Jew who was being beaten up by an Egyptian. In the attempt he killed the Egyptian and as a result had to flee from Pharaoh's anger. He ended up in the desert far from the comforts of palace life and spent forty years doing the lonely job of looking after sheep. But the desert achieved something a palace never could: it killed the arrogance in Moses. Eventually God called him to return to Egypt and lead his people out of their slavery and into the promised land. By this time Moses was a changed man, and instead of relying on his palace training and natural abilities, he confessed to feeling totally inadequate for the task. He demonstrated a poverty of spirit, which was probably why God chose him. Later in the story of Israel's escape from Egypt via the Red Sea, Moses was described as a very humble man, more humble than anyone else on the face of the earth. Yet he became one of the greatest leaders of all time.

It seems that what success and ease cannot produce, failure and suffering can. The resulting humility is highly valued by God – in fact in His economy only the meek are fit to inherit the earth which He created. They are the only ones He can entrust with such a task, because they know their own weakness and will rely on God's help to do the job.

## THEME – A HUNGER FOR RIGHTEOUSNESS

### Materials:

Some blown up pictures of starving people from one of the drought-blighted countries of Africa. Some water biscuits.

### Talk:

Probably none of us here knows what it is like to be starving like these poor people in Africa (show the pictures). Most of us have a refrigerator full of food, and even if the bread runs out we have some biscuits in the cupboard (show the biscuits). It is hard for us to comprehend what it must be like to suffer with painful hunger pangs.

It is good to be a careful housekeeper and have something in the cupboard to fall back on, but it is not good to allow an attitude of complacency to extend to our spiritual lives, so that we never allow ourselves to feel hungry for God.

### Reading: Matthew 5:6

Jesus once told a story about a man who had the nerve to wake up his neighbour in the middle of the night and ask him for bread. Apparently a visitor had descended on him and he had no bread in the house to offer him after his long journey. His neighbour was in bed with his family and did not want to be disturbed, but the man persevered and kept knocking and begging for the bread. Eventually, for the sake of peace, the neighbour got up and gave him the bread so that his family could get back to sleep (Luke 11:5–8).

The only reason this man was prepared to go to all that trouble, and suffer the embarrassment of waking his neighbour, was because he literally had nothing in his cupboard – not even a dry biscuit – and he knew his neighbour had bread. Perhaps he had smelled it baking the previous evening.

In the Western world self-reliance is encouraged. We don't like to be dependent on others or to come across as weak and needy. So we hardly ever admit to being spiritually or emotionally hungry.

Jesus said that it is the hungry who are to be envied – those who hunger and thirst for righteousness – those who want to know God better – those who want to grow spiritually – those who want to become more like Jesus; the sort of people who are so desperate for God that they will not leave Him alone, but keep on knocking on the doors of Heaven. They are starving for God as the people in those pictures are starving for food. Jesus said that they are the ones who will be filled.

Everyone gets pangs of spiritual hunger, but most of us tend to satisfy the pangs with TV, something to eat, other people, a good book – anything which will momentarily meet the need. If we want to be filled with the good things from Heaven, first we need to know that we are empty. Secondly we need to know that God has food which truly satisfies. When we know these two things we will have the energy and audacity to keep knocking until God answers our prayer.

## THEME – MERCY AND PEACE

*Materials:*

Game of Monopoly, the card 'Get out of jail free'. A rough wooden cross placed where everyone can see it.

*Reading: Matthew 5:7, 9*

*Talk:*

In our society we rarely experience mercy; criticisms and 'put downs' are far more common. But mercy and peace permeate God's Kingdom. In fact it is a Kingdom founded on mercy, and the air you breathe is peace. None of us could enter its gates without God's mercy operating in our lives. Someone has said that grace is getting what we don't deserve and mercy is not getting what we do deserve. We deserve punishment for breaking God's laws, but God showed us mercy by allowing Jesus, His precious, sinless son, to take our punishment instead of us. The cross is where justice and mercy come together. It was on the cross that God made peace with us. It is as if we have a 'Get out of jail free' card permanently in our pocket (show the card). During a game of Monopoly you may pick up this card and keep it in case you ever land in jail. Should this happen you will be able to get out of jail without payment.

*Discussion:*

In what ways can we show mercy?

When we receive mercy we are obligated to pass it on to others. We demonstrate mercy and peace in two ways. First through forgiveness and then by alleviating suffering wherever possible. We are called to be like Christ, who forgave those who crucified him. Jesus taught us to pray: 'Forgive us, our debts, [sins] as we have forgiven our debtors [those who have sinned against us].' It seems that our receiving mercy is conditional on giving it to others, which is a sobering thought. How many times, I wonder, have we used the words: 'It's unforgivable', or 'I can never forgive them'. Releasing forgiveness to those who have hurt us is hard for us all. Children do it very reluctantly, and usually only because they have been forced to do so by their parents. But it is important for our own spiritual health and healing that we do so. When we refuse to forgive someone it is as if we are chained to that person. Once we have forgiven we are free to move on.

The second way we show mercy and bring peace is when we try to alleviate the suffering of others. Mother Theresa was a shining example for us. Her whole life was spent showing mercy to the outcasts of society; those who were considered untouchable by others.

We have all been called to a ministry of mercy and peace. It may not be on the streets of Calcutta, but right where we live, whenever we meet suffering and discord. There are many people who cross our paths daily to whom we could show mercy, even perhaps bringing some peace into their lives.

# THEME – SINCERITY

## *Materials:*

One jar of 'light' chocolate drink and one jar of ordinary chocolate drink. (Check that the calorie content is more or less the same on both.)

## *Talk:*

Many people today are on low-fat diets. They are anxious to lose weight or to cut down their cholesterol intake, so they buy foods with a 'light' label (like this chocolate drink). Sadly, the labelling is misleading. The product may have less fat but when the calorie content is examined in the light chocolate you discover that it is almost the same as that of the ordinary chocolate. Yes, there is less fat, but it has more sugar to enhance the taste. The manufacturers are not exactly dishonest but they are more concerned about getting your money than keeping you healthy, so their labelling often lacks integrity.

Sincerity and integrity are rare but precious commodities. It is especially important that children see integrity in their parents' lives. There is nothing more disappointing and disillusioning to children than parents who do not keep their word, or who resort to lying. (Give an example of your own, or tell the following story.)

There is a sad story told by a man whose young sons longed for a pet dog. One day they found a stray and asked their father if

96

they could keep it. It didn't seem to belong to anyone so the father agreed. The dog was a very ordinary 'Heinz 57' brand of mongrel. The only thing which made it distinctive was three white hairs in its tail. The children had the dog for several weeks and had grown to love him, when an advert appeared in the local paper appealing for the return of a lost dog with the distinguishing mark of three white hairs in its tail. A neighbour answered the advert, saying that she had seen such a dog. So the owner called to see the dog and check if it was his. The children were upset at the thought of losing their pet, and their father, wanting to please his boys, pulled out the offending hairs before the owner arrived. Although the dog ran to him and greeted him with obvious delight, finding no white hairs in the tail the disappointed owner left the dog behind. The father ended his story saying that the family kept the dog, but he lost his integrity and his sons lost their faith.

### Reading: Matthew 5:8

To be pure in heart means to be sincere. The word 'sincere' comes from the Latin 'sin cera', meaning 'without wax'. In Roman times sellers of marble would place a notice on a slab of marble saying it was 'sincere'. The slab was exactly what it seemed. No one had rubbed wax into the cracks to disguise them. Jesus said the sincere would be happy because they would see God. Nothing would cloud their vision of God. They were not cluttered up with mixed motives. The pure in heart have a childlike simplicity about their faith. What motivates them is their desire for God and His Kingdom, and to such people God makes Himself available.

## THEME – COURAGE

*Materials:*

Write to Christian Solidarity Worldwide, PO Box 99, New Malden, Surrey, KT3 3YF (Tel. 020 8942 8810), and ask for some posters and newsletters about persecuted Christians in other countries. Arrange these on a board for all to see.

*Reading: Matthew 5:10–11*

*Talk:*

Christians throughout the ages have been persecuted for their faith. Daniel's three friends were put into a fiery furnace because they would not bow down to an idol. The early Christians were thrown to the lions because of their belief in Jesus. During the Reformation, Latimer, Ridley and Cranmer were burnt at the stake in Oxford for their beliefs. A cross in The Broad marks the spot to this day. Until recently Christians in the Soviet Union were imprisoned for their faith. Today, as we sit here Christians in various parts of the world are suffering terrible persecution. (Show the posters from Christian Solidarity, and pick out some stories of persecution.)

When we hear these stories and think about the men and women who have suffered, even to the point of death, on account of their faith, we wonder how we would have fared under the same circumstances. The Romanian Christian, Richard Wurmbrand, was held by communists for fourteen years in solitary confinement. He was kept in a tiny cell in which he could barely move. Yet in that cell he spent many a night dancing for joy.[10] The guards, seeing Richard Wurmbrand dancing, must have wondered how he could be so happy in such terrible circumstances. They would have counted him a miserable, most unfortunate prisoner. How then could he have experienced such joy? In that cell Wurmbrand received a foretaste of the freedom and joy that is now his in Heaven.

We may never experience prison or the threat of death for our faith, but there are other forms of persecution which we may have to face.

### Discussion:

Ask the group to share a time when they have suffered in some way for their faith.

Sometimes when we become Christians we have to put up with some ridicule from our families and friends, and that can be painful. It may be an issue of morality which causes others to scorn us. People have been known to lose their jobs because they have not been prepared to go along with a dishonest practice at work. It can be quite hard to own up to being a Christian in today's climate, and many of us have felt guilty for our lack of courage. Do you remember how the frightened disciples remained hidden away in an upper room after the crucifixion? Then on the day of Pentecost God poured out His Holy Spirit upon them and they were filled with courage and boldness. Let's pray that God will fill us with His Holy Spirit so that we will have the courage to endure whatever persecution comes our way, and in the process have a foretaste, like the late Richard Wurmbrand, of Glory Divine.

# CHAPTER SIX

# GLIMPSES OF JESUS

I am the way the truth and the life.
Before Abraham I was.

## THEME – GETTING TO KNOW JESUS

### Materials:

A man's handkerchief and five matches. Push four of the matches secretly into the hem of the handkerchief. Keep the fifth.

### Talk:

Ask the group if they have ever tried their hand at magic, or, watched a really clever magician at work. 'Now you see it – Now you don't!' One minute the coin is in the hand, the next it is gone and then it appears from behind someone's ear.

### Action:

Take the handkerchief and place the fifth match in the centre of it, for all to see. Fold it up but select a match in the hem, hold it out, then ask someone to break it. Open up the handkerchief and produce the other match still whole. You can do this another three times with others in the group. (Use another trick if you prefer.) Then reveal how the trick is done.

It seems like magic, but of course it's just trickery. It is momentarily baffling but once it is explained it is all too simple.

Tell the group the story of Moses in the desert. Many years ago a shepherd was looking after his sheep in the desert when something strange caught his eye. He could hardly believe what he was seeing. A bush was on fire, but it was not burning up. He went closer and something even stranger occurred. A voice spoke to him from within the bush and called his name. 'Moses, Moses . . . Do not come any closer. Take off your sandals, for the place where you are standing is holy ground'(Exodus 3:5). This was no magic trick! This was supernatural – this was God!

Magicians may be able to amaze us for a short while, but there is nothing supernatural about what they do. Only God is supernatural. Only He can get around the laws of nature that He created.

During this encounter with Moses God disclosed His own name – 'I AM'. This became the sacred name by which the Israelites knew their God. It described God's nature. He who was, and is, and is to come. He is the everlasting, ever present, all powerful, all knowing God. So sacred was this name that the Israelites dared not even pronounce it aloud. They considered it blasphemous to do so. Imagine, then, how horrified the religious authorities must have been when they heard Jesus use the very same words: 'I AM' to describe Himself.

### Reading: John 8:58

Everyone who heard those words knew that Jesus was declaring Himself to be God. That was why they wanted to stone Him for blasphemy. Not only did Jesus say that He was God, but also that if people really knew Him they would also know His Father in Heaven.

### Discussion:

Ask the group to think about some of their friends. How quickly and easily did they get to know them?

Communication is the key to intimacy. Before we can really know another person that person has to share a little about himself or herself. Well, Jesus shared Himself with His disciples and using the sacred title of 'I am' he gave them insights into His character. As they got to know Him they got to know His Father in Heaven. In the same way, as we get to know Jesus, we are getting to know His Father.

## THEME – I AM THE BREAD OF LIFE

### *Materials:*

One loaf of bread, one bag of sweets.

### *Talk:*

Everyone has needs that demand satisfaction. There are physical needs for food, water and warmth, which for us are fairly easily met. We can pass by the baker and buy one of these. (Hold up the loaf of bread.) Tragically, there are many millions in the world, even today, who are without these basic necessities of life. But in the West we are privileged to have our primary needs satisfied, which means we can attend to other needs which surface at varying times in life.

### *Reading: John 6:35–40*

(Move from talking about physical needs to emotional and spiritual ones.) It may seem odd for Jesus to liken Himself to a loaf of bread. But what do we do with bread? (Hold up the bread, break it and eat a piece.) We break it and eat it. It satisfies our hunger and sustains our lives. Our first needs are the physical ones, but after that we have emotional and spiritual needs which also cry out to be met. Maybe you long to feel secure and loved. Or you want to be valued by others and to feel good about yourself. Or maybe you want to achieve something of significance. Perhaps one of these is your personal inner hunger. Hunger demands satisfaction. Sadly, too often we seek to meet our needs with stuff that does us no good – like junk food which offers no real nourishment. (Hold up the bag of sweets.) We look for our security in material things; we look for our value reflected in other people's eyes; we look for our significance in how well we perform. But we are looking at the wrong things to satisfy our needs. Jesus says: 'I am the bread of life . . . come to me and you will never be hungry again. I can be your security. I can give you value. I can provide you with significance.'

In third world countries a loaf of bread would keep people alive physically. In the West we are well looked after physically, but what about our spiritual needs? Many of us are dying of spiritual hunger. Jesus says He is the living bread. He is the sustaining power of our spiritual life. There can be no substitute. If we feed on Him we will live forever.

### Discussion:

How can we feed on Jesus?

The first thing to do is stop filling ourselves up with junk food. We wouldn't let our children eat sweets just before a meal and then expect them to enjoy their dinner. Neither should we take the edge off our hunger for God by snacking on stuff that does us no good. Secondly we must feed on Him by spending time with Him. His presence marvellously fills that empty space inside us. Lastly, our hunger is especially satisfied when we obey Him. It was after a long, dusty journey and a conversation with a woman at a well that Jesus gave us insight into what satisfied Him. He said: 'My food is to do the will of Him who sent me and to finish His work.' When we seek to do God's will, which could be taking time out of a busy day to talk to a lonely or needy person, we will find that the bread not only satisfies but comes with jam on it. Nothing is more fulfilling and sweeter than doing the will of God.

## THEME – I AM THE LIGHT OF THE WORLD

*Materials:*

A packet of small self-igniting candles, one ordinary candle.

*Talk:*

We are twenty-first century, Western women who take light for granted. We are used to having electricity at the touch of a switch. We live our lives trusting in light to guide us, to enable us to work during the winter months, to travel in the hours of darkness, to get up and feed the baby in the middle of the night – we would be lost without it. Can you remember what it is like to have a power cut? The first thing you do is to look for some candles to provide you with alternative light. Just in case the Y2K Bug caused the electricity to fail, most people stocked up on candles for the beginning of the new millennium.

(Light a candle.) The problem with candles, and to a degree with electricity, is that they can fail. Candles burn down, or blow out. Like this one (blow it out). Electric generators can be blown up, cables can be blown down and in a moment we can be plunged into darkness. What we need is something that doesn't fail – something like these candles – a light that will not go out however hard we blow it.

(Light the self-igniting candles and try to blow them out.)

We have of course been talking about physical light, which is very important to us. But however necessary it is, it isn't as vital as spiritual light. It is annoying or even worrying when the electricity fails and we can't find the candles, but it is even more distressing to be in the dark spiritually. Family life is full of joys, heartaches, hard work and problems. We need more than just human wisdom and strength to get us through. Sometimes life is lonely and we need someone alongside who loves us, with whom we can talk and who will never let us down. Sooner or later we all have to face people close to us becoming ill and even dying, and eventually we have to face our own mortality. It must be frightening to face that with no assurance of a life after death.

### Reading: John 8:12

Someone once said: 'A blind man who sees is better than a seeing man who is blind.'

We can have all the electric light or candles we need, and yet be in darkness. Living without Jesus to light the way for us is a bit like living in a house wired up to the electricity supply and not knowing how to switch it on. We were specially made to have a relationship with the living God; to be connected to Him through Jesus Christ. The wonderful thing about Jesus is that He never fails. A hurricane won't interfere with the supply. Nothing can blow Him out, nor burn Him down, like a candle. His light is everlasting and will be there to light the way in the worst storms, the darkest night, and the most testing times of our lives.

The late King George VI will be remembered for a quote by Minnie Louise Haskins that he once used: 'And I said to the man who stood at the gate of the year "Give me a light that I may tread safely into the unknown," and he said; "Go out into the darkness and put your hand into the hand of God. That shall be to you better than light and better than a known way." '[11]

## THEME – I AM THE GATE AND THE SHEPHERD

### Materials:

Articles that make children and adults feel secure e.g. dummy, fluffy blanket, night light, padlock and chain, Valentine's card, £20 note. A tape recording of 'The Lord is my Shepherd' (Psalm 23).

### Talk:

For all of us security is high on the agenda. We all need to feel safe and secure. Some of us can remember times when we have felt very insecure indeed.

### Discussion:

Show the group the various articles you have brought – things that make both children and adults feel safe. Then ask them to think about the particular things that make them feel secure. Or what they do when they feel insecure. Ask two or three to share their thoughts with the group.

### Reading: John 10:11–14

In New Testament times a shepherd stayed with his sheep day and night. During the day he would lead them out to find luscious green grass to eat. At night he would take them back to the pen, probably erected out of stones, and when the sheep were all safely inside he would lay himself down in the gap, where a gate would have been, ready to protect them against thieves and robbers or wild animals.

First Jesus referred to Himself as a gate, which to us conjures up a picture of a strong, solid, unyielding, cold and rather inanimate object. But Jesus' disciples would have pictured a country shepherd who had been hardened by the elements and, armed with his staff, was capable of preventing wolves and robbers from attacking his precious flock. Secondly Jesus referred to Himself as a shepherd. He was not just a defence preventing harm reaching the sheep, but He also actively cared for them. To the disciples' minds a gate and a shepherd would be synonymous with looking after sheep.

Life has always had its cares. Anxiety and stress was probably as much of a problem 2000 years ago as it is today, though perhaps it came about for different reasons. Jesus was reassuring His followers that He would take care of them. He is God who became man, and was put under the same pressures that all human beings experience. He knows and understands our need to feel secure and in this passage He is reassuring his followers, down through the ages, that He will be there for them – day and night. In fact He is more dependable than all the things we use to make ourselves feel safe. (Finish by playing the tape of 'The Lord is my Shepherd'.)

## Theme – I am the Resurrection and the Life

### Materials:

A handful of seeds, and fruit from the mature plants into which they grow. For example, a tomato seed and a tomato, an apple pip and an apple, a grain of wheat and a head of wheat.

### Activity:

Hand the seeds around for the group to identify. Then give them the fruit to match the two together.

### Talk:

When a seed is buried in the earth it is like a death and a resurrection. First it is buried, then time passes and something amazing happens, secretly, beneath the soil. The seed has disintegrated, rooted and then begun to sprout. First a very small shoot appears – like a resurrection. It continues to grow and eventually becomes a plant which ripens and produces fruit.

Death is rather an alarming subject to most of us. None of us likes to think too much about our own death. If we knew for sure that after death we would go on existing, maybe with a spiritual body, though in essence the same, we could probably cope with it. Like this tomato (show the seed and the lovely red tomato). One comes out of the other, and yet they look so different. Perhaps the change is easier for us to comprehend when we think of the caterpillar becoming a chrysalis and eventually emerging as a beautiful butterfly.

*Reading: John 11:25*

After Jesus had said this He went to the tomb of His friend Lazarus, who had died three days previously, and raised him from the dead. First He made that unbelievable and astounding statement about being the resurrection, and then proved to everyone that He was speaking the truth. All the miracles that Jesus did were signs of the Kingdom of God which was yet to come in its fullness. When God's Kingdom has fully come there will be no more sickness, so He healed the sick as a sign of that. When Jesus finally brings in God's Kingdom in fullness and glory there will be no more death. The dead will be raised with a new body; one that can never grow old and sick and die again. So in one sense this miracle was like a 'dress rehearsal'.

The tomb of Lazarus was a dark, dank hole. Imagine the astonishment of the crowd when Jesus cried out: 'Lazarus come out!' And they watched the dead man come out still wrapped in his grave clothes. Raising Lazarus from the dead was a way of giving us visible proof that what He said was true – that He really is the resurrection and the life for all those who believe in Him.

But His crowning proof was His own death and resurrection. Just in case people were still in doubt after He had raised Lazarus, there was the resurrection of Christ Himself after He had been put to death by the Roman authorities. Over forty days He appeared to many different people in a recognisable form. So Jesus not only told us that He was the resurrection and the life, but He proved it to us, so that we need never be alarmed by the fear of death.

## THEME – I AM THE WAY, THE TRUTH AND THE LIFE

### Materials:

A road map of the country, photo album, school textbook, TV magazine, a fashion magazine.

### Activity:

Ask the group to suggest a route from where they are to a town about two hundred miles away. Then check it with the road map and see how close they have come to the best route.

### Talk:

Explain that we all need maps to help us find the way to places. We also need help to find the best way to live our lives. Show the group the things which people generally use to model their lives on. Photo of parents, school book, media, etc.

### Discussion:

Ask the group who they modelled their lives on when they were growing up.

When we want to travel to a place we have never visited before, we usually need a map to follow. In the same way children, as they grow up, consciously or unconsciously look for signposts – people who will point the way. We all tend to model ourselves on those we admire or are close to. Not all our models have been good ones. Some of us have reached adulthood and are still searching for a good pattern for our lives.

*Reading: John 14:1–7*

In this passage Jesus told His disciples He was going to leave them and go to His Father's house to prepare a place for them, so that they could be with Him. But He didn't tell them how to get there. When they asked for a route He didn't give them lots of alternatives, such as the quick route, the scenic route, or the country route, He gave them only one – which must have completely baffled them. He said that He was the Way. He is the road to His Father's house. In fact no one gets there unless they go through Him. But not only is Jesus the way to eternal life; He is also the supreme example for our life on earth and the one upon whom we should model our lives.

Jesus is also the Truth. Twenty-first century people live in a world where they assume there are no absolute truths. We are told that we have a right to happiness and the right to do whatever will make us feel fulfilled and good about ourselves. We can believe in horoscopes, crystals, even reincarnation. It's a world where your opinion is as good as the next person's opinion. But Jesus says that He is the truth, not deception; absolute, not relative; trustworthy, not unreliable; the ultimate reality, not virtual reality.

Jesus will show us the way to live while we are here on earth. He has the answers to all of life's spiritual, and philosophical questions. He is not only the way to life and the truth about life, but He is Life itself. He is the one who has gone before and opened the way to Heaven for us.

## THEME – I AM THE TRUE VINE, YOU ARE THE BRANCHES

### *Materials:*

A branch and some secateurs.

### *Talk:*

(Explain that all shrubs need pruning.) I wonder if you have shrubs in your garden which need pruning every year? You walk around the garden snipping here and there (take the secateurs and cut a twig off the branch). You think nothing of cutting back the roses, knowing that the blooms will be more prolific later if you do.

### *Reading: John 15:1–6*

A branch like this one (hold up the branch) cannot produce fruit any more because there is no sap, no goodness coming through. Detached from the main stem it is as good as dead. In this passage Jesus describes Himself as the main stem, or the true vine. Only the branches which are attached to Him will bear fruit. Jesus wanted us to know that without Him we could do nothing. The real fruits of the Spirit – love, joy, peace, patience, kindness, goodness, faithfulness, gentleness and self-control are impossible to produce without the Spirit of Jesus in our lives. Not only that, but we will gradually cease to bear fruit unless we are pruned regularly. Any shrub will grow straggly and untidy unless the gardener comes along with his pruning scissors.

But God isn't exactly going to appear to us one afternoon, with a pair of secateurs in His hand. Is He? So how does He prune us?

Think for a moment of something that happened during this last week, which really irritated, hurt, even angered you. (Give the group time to think and share.) Perhaps it was the 'neighbours from hell', the overactive, even disobedient child, the unreliable friend, the car that broke down, or the lawn that should have been cut, but wasn't. (Give a personal example.) These are God's ways of pruning us. 'But how can they be?' you say, 'when they are just stupid irritations?' Imagine an up and coming young tennis player whose ambition is to play at Wimbledon, but his backhand is weak. Do you think the tennis coach ignores the backhand and keeps sending the practice balls to his forehand because it's easier for the young man? No, he will continually send balls down the court to his backhand because practice makes perfect. If we want to grow in patience, kindness and endurance then we must be prepared to be tested continually in these areas.

King Saul was the first King of Israel. He was a handsome, tall young man, but gradually became arrogant, proud and jealous of other people's success. God was displeased with Saul and chose young David to be king instead. David was anointed when he was a teenager but didn't become king until Saul died. During the fifteen years of waiting David was hounded from pillar to post by Saul, who wanted to kill him. Someone has suggested that God used the outer Saul to kill the inner Saul in David. David could have become just like Saul, but during the years of hardship God was pruning him so that when he came to the throne his reign was remembered as the best time in Israel's history.

Two things will produce good fruit in our lives: staying attached to the stem and being pruned by the gardener.

# CHAPTER SEVEN

# RELATIONSHIPS

Friendship improves happiness, and abates misery, by doubling our joy and dividing our grief. (Joseph Addison, 1672–1719)

## THEME – THE BLESSINGS OF FRIENDSHIP

God did not mean us to live in isolation from others. Yet the world is full of many lonely people.

### Discussion:

(Discuss with the group why some find it hard to form lasting relationships.)

### Talk:

Perhaps our twenty-first century way of life is largely to blame. No longer are we born, grow up, then work and marry in the same community. Now families move frequently, and end up living in different parts of the country, even on different continents. This mobility militates against lasting, stable relationships. Casual, brief attachments become the order of the day. There is also a radical individualism abroad, which means people opt to live alone rather than share their lives with others. Another factor which keeps some from entering into close relationships, especially if they come from broken homes, is fear – fear of the possible loss and hurt which could be involved if they dare to enter the challenging arena of friendship. So people stay lonely.

But 'no man is an island', as the poet John Donne said. Men and women were created for relationships.

### Reading: Ecclesiastes 4:9–12

1. There is gain to be found in friendship. Pleasure is multiplied and trouble is halved when they are shared with others.

2. Our relationships provide support. We all go through difficulties and at times need a listening ear. It is sad that many people prefer to pay a stranger to listen to their woes rather than use the natural God-given provision for support and healing – a friend.
3. Friends are comforting and strengthening. The world can be a hostile place. It is easier to face the challenges of life with someone else than on one's own. When we get wounded a friend helps to bind up our wounds, and vice versa.
4. A good friendship should be challenging. We all need someone who will hold up a mirror for us to see ourselves as others see us. It is easy to live in ignorance of our irritating habits. Wounds from a friend can be trusted (Proverbs 27:6).

Bearing in mind the advantages of a good friendship, perhaps we need to take steps to become more friendly and develop the qualities needed to maintain healthy and mutually beneficial relationships.

### Discussion:

What qualities would members of the group look for in a friend?

The fact is we can't lose if we put time and effort into relationships. But it does take commitment. Something as good as friendship is not usually made and maintained without effort. It may be entered into fairly easily but a commitment is necessary to survive the testing times. The Bible reveals many interesting relationships. Most of them are tested in the furnace of difficulty and hammered out on the anvil of time.

## THEME – COMMITMENT

*Materials:*

Two wedding rings.

*Talk:*

Friendship may exist between people of the same sex, or within a marriage relationship. A marriage based on friendship is one more likely to endure. Sadly these days our relationships tend to be like any other commodity – not built to last. A hundred years ago one bought a carpet, or a suit, or some saucepans to last a lifetime. Family and friends were also there for the long haul. They stuck by each other through thick and thin.

One famous Bible relationship was that between David and Jonathan.

*Reading: 1 Samuel 18:1–4*

David and Jonathan met after David had killed Goliath and it seems that they were immediately drawn to one another and made a covenant with one another. A covenant is like a commitment. It binds two people together with promises that they both make. To mark it they give something of themselves to each other. In a marriage we exchange rings as a symbol of the binding agreement (show the rings). In this instance Jonathan gave David his robe, his tunic, his sword, his bow and his belt. It would seem that Jonathan had recognised that David was more suited to be king than he was, even though he was the heir to the throne. So in this gesture he symbolically handed over to David his right to reign. In return David assured him of lifelong friendship and promised to look after Jonathan's family.

### Reading: 1 Samuel 20:41–42

The two men were eventually forced to part, because David needed to escape from King Saul's threats. The parting was heart-rending. Once more they swore lifelong friendship in God's name, and re-affirmed the covenant between the two families. When finally Saul and Jonathan were killed David sang a lament for them both, but had a special song for Jonathan: 'Jonathan lies slain on your heights. I grieve for you, Jonathan my brother; you were very dear to me. Your love for me was wonderful, more wonderful than that of women' (2 Samuel 1:25–26).

This was a beautiful and lasting friendship. It was marked by a covenant to love one another and to be there for each other. Isn't this the sort of relationship we would value? It may be impracticable, unless it is within marriage, to expect such a binding commitment from a friend. But perhaps we could learn to be there for our friends in a more committed manner than before.

### Discussion:

What sort of commitment would be practical to expect from a friend today?

## THEME – WORKING TOGETHER

*Talk:*

(Give your own illustration of working together to get a job done or use the following.)

Some of us enjoy watching 'Ground Force' on TV. In the programme a number of people descend on someone's garden to give it a makeover. Alan Titchmarsh is the brain behind the scheme. Charlie Dimmock, the lady who can dig like a man, specialises in water features. Tommy Walsh, besides being Mr Muscle Man, is an expert in carpentry and cementing. Then, of course, the job would never get done without the tea maker who makes him or herself responsible for lifting the team's energy levels with constant beverages. Together all these people remake a garden in a few days, and finish in the nick of time to surprise the delighted owner. Alone the task would be impossible. Together a miracle can occur!

*Reading: 1 Corinthians 12:12,27*

St Paul likens the church to a body. Every part has its separate function, but it works together to extend God's Kingdom.

In order to talk to you my mind has to think what to say. It has to instruct my hands to hold the book, my eyes to read the words and my mouth to utter them, then my ears double check to see if what I have said sounds all right. The body works in unison to get the job done. Paul implies that the church works best in this way.

### Reading: Exodus 17:10–13

Thousands of Israelites won the battle against the Amalekites. Four men in particular are mentioned: Joshua, Moses, Aaron and Hur. Joshua did the fighting on the ground and Moses went up on the hill over looking the battlefield. As long as he held his hands up to God the Israelites were winning. When he tired and lowered them they began to lose. So Aaron and Hur came to his rescue and held up his hands so that finally Joshua overcame the Amalekites. Together they were victorious.

Whether it is in our secular lives or in the life of the church, we function best in relationship with other people. Our struggles, our tasks, our challenges are facilitated by other people being given the opportunity to help us in different ways. There are occasions when we urgently need support, but sometimes we are too proud to ask for it and miss out on a God-ordained means of blessing. Solomon once said: 'Two are better than one, because they have a good return for their work' (Ecclesiastes 4:9).

Giving and receiving from one another is a skill we need to cultivate.

## THEME – DISCIPLINE MADE EASY

### Materials:

Pieces of broccoli and cauliflower; a bar of chocolate and a packet of biscuits.

### Talk:

Ask the group which is easier, to attempt to diet on one's own, or to do it with others.

Imagine if two of you have chosen to go on a forty-day fast, abstaining from everything except fruit and vegetables. Everyone else is eating normally and they insensitively eat chocolate and biscuits right in front of you. (Offer the vegetable pieces to two people and the sweet things to the others.) How does it make you feel?

It is hard to discipline ourselves, especially when it comes to giving up something we really enjoy, even when it is for our own good – such as giving up smoking, or sweets. Alone it could be very hard, but making a pact with others and agreeing to stand together makes it easier.

### Reading: Daniel 1:1–17

Here four young Jewish men had been taken into exile and were being trained for service in King Nebuchadnezzar's household. As Jews many of the foods they were offered were forbidden to them, so they asked to be put on a very plain diet. It must have been a hard decision to make and even harder to keep. The shared commitment gave them the strength to persevere and withstand the disapproval of others.

The Christian life often calls for discipline and courage. When we are alone it is hard to maintain the spiritual disciplines which help us to be salt and light in the world. It is like taking a hot ember out of the fire and placing it on its own in the grate. While the other embers keep burning the lone coal will gradually dim and finally die out. Christians are the same. We need one another's support and encouragement to keep alive.

We should do all we can to maintain contact with our family and friends who are not part of the church fellowship. At the same time we need friends around us who have the same values and ideals, so that we can stand together and encourage one another, like Daniel and his friends.

*Talk:*

(Either give your own example of encouragement or use the following.)

An American pastor called Ken Blue once told the story of a visit he paid to his grandfather's farm in North Minnesota when he was about five years old. His grandfather had taken him for a ride on one of the farm carthorses, which was so huge that his little legs could hardly straddle its back. His grandfather had taken him slowly around the paddock and then looked up at his grandson and said: 'Kenny boy you are a natural.' The comment left its mark. From that moment on Ken Blue believed himself to be a natural horseman. He never mounted a horse again until he was twenty-one and in the army. He entered the US Modern Pentathlon, and one of the events was equestrian jumping. He was undaunted by the fact that he had no experience. He was sure of his natural ability. In 1968 he participated in the Olympic Games in Mexico City.[12]

*Talk:*

Some parents and school teachers believe that criticism makes children work harder. It usually has quite the opposite effect. A child works far better in an atmosphere of encouragement than in one of discouragement. In fact we all need encouragement and can find new vision, energy and resources when we have it.

*Reading: Acts 4:36; 9:26,27; 11:22–26; 15:36–38*

Barnabas was really called Joseph, but the apostles renamed him Barnabas because the name meant 'son of encouragement'. Barnabas was noted for that important gift of encouragement. How fortunate his friends were to have someone like him around. They must have loved his company. One of his friends was the apostle Paul. Paul tried to join the disciples in Jerusalem but found it difficult. Everyone was suspicious of him because he had previously persecuted the Christians so cruelly. But Barnabas took him under his wing and introduced him to the apostles. He also took him on his first ministry trip to Antioch and started him on the ministry for which he was to become famous. Sadly Paul and Barnabas eventually fell out because Barnabas, true to his name, decided to stick by a young friend in trouble. This was John Mark, who had been with them when he had become frightened by the persecution they met and run away. Because of this Paul wanted to leave him behind, but Barnabas knew that it would discourage John Mark even more and simply be rubbing salt into the wound. So he insisted that John Mark be allowed to come. It was then that Barnabas and Paul separated.

We need friends who will encourage us, especially when we are going through a tough time. Some of us are very good at using very negative self-talk. We often become our own worst enemies, condemning ourselves when we think we may have made a mistake, or done something stupid. We really don't need friends who will confirm our own worst fears. Instead we need people around who will encourage us to get up and try again. Barnabas didn't deny that Paul had been a persecutor of the church, but he wanted to give him the opportunity to prove his change of heart and sincerity to the apostles. Nor did he deny that John Mark had failed them, but he knew how important it

ENCOURAGEMENT 133

was that John Mark received the encouragement of being given a second chance.

None of us need telling when we have made a mistake. What we need are friends who believe in us enough to give us a second chance. How wonderful if we could all merit the nickname Barnabas (daughter of encouragement).

## Theme – Shared interests

*Materials:*

Photographs, or postcards of some beautiful scenery.

*Activity:*

Hand the photos and cards around, and then ask the group to say who they would like to visit those places with. (Most will probably suggest their husband, but some might name a friend.)

*Talk:*

Someone has said that it's love that keeps the marriage going round. In fact it is marriage that keeps the love going round. In other words it is not so much love that keeps commitment alive, it is the commitment to the relationship which keeps the love alive.

After a few years of marriage it is only too easy for couples to drift apart. Most of the day is spent apart and the evenings are often taken up with the family and household chores. The busyness and weariness of family life can be overwhelming. It takes determination to keep the relationship from deteriorating – leaving two separate people leading separate lives under the same roof. One of the important commitments within a marriage relationship or a friendship is the commitment to share – sharing interests and activities together. Boredom is an enemy to any relationship. Common interests and having fun together keeps the relationship alive and fresh.

### Reading: Acts 18:1–4,18,24,26; Romans 16:3; 1 Corinthians 16:19

Whenever Aquila and Priscilla's names are mentioned in Scripture they are always together. They gave hospitality to Paul together, they travelled together, they counselled Apollos together, and also ran a church together. They had a real partnership. They were doing something they both loved and believed in together, and yet able to express their distinctive gifts within that activity.

One of the best ways of building a friendship, or a marriage, is through shared interests, especially performing some sort of service together. Jesus deliberately sent his disciples on ministry trips two by two. In this way they were able to support each other, help each other and enjoy the experience together.

Shared activities cement a relationship. C.S. Lewis writes that friendship must be about something even if it were only an enthusiasm for dominoes or white mice. Those who have nothing can share nothing; those who are going nowhere can have no fellow-travellers.[13]

Certainly Aquila and Priscilla had a common interest in furthering the gospel, which was mutually absorbing. One of the most fulfilling and rewarding activities is to serve God and others together.

### Discussion:

First ask the group to list some of the different activities they share with spouse or friend. Then they should list activities they

could do which would involve them in serving others together.
Examples could include:

Giving hospitality to lonely people
Opening their home to a cell (home) group
Leading a cell group together
Visiting the prisons together
Doing a soup run for the homeless living on the streets.

*Talk:*

Communication must be a vital ingredient in any friendship. There are three stages to it: talking, listening and understanding. It is easy to talk and not be heard, as many wives have discovered when they have tried to tell their husbands something in bed at night. Instead of grunts, denoting a listening ear, their words have been greeted with deep breathing and even the hint of a snore!

However, our friend or spouse may have spoken to us and we may have heard the words but that does not mean the communication has been understood. We all bring our personal history into our relationships and expect another person who is ignorant of that history to intuitively understand all we say. For example, a person brought up in a rural environment may suggest to her friend or spouse that they get away from it all for the weekend, with a country retreat in mind. The friend, though he or she agrees, may have been brought up in the city and have something more suburban in mind. When communicating with our friends we have to learn to listen well and then through question and answer, if necessary, reach an understanding.

But communication is more than just conversation; touch and eye contact are two other powerful means of communication. One imparts a lot through eye contact.

*Activity:*

Ask someone to convey a strong emotion using just her eyes and let the others guess what the emotion is.

Touch is also an important way of communicating with our friends. We all need a hug now and again. In fact touch has been scientifically proven to benefit our health. Back in the 1920s a doctor by the name of Fritz Talbot introduced a concept called 'Tender Loving Care' into the foundling hospitals in the USA. Up until then the death rate in these hospitals had been extremely high. While visiting a clinic in Dusseldorf, Germany, he had noticed a fat old woman carrying a very measly baby around on her hip. When he asked what the old lady was doing he was told that when a baby was sick and all medical remedies had been tried, then they gave it to 'Old Anna' and she was always successful.[14]

### Reading: John 15:15

Jesus saw communication as a mark of friendship. His friends were those to whom He communicated the things He had learned from His Father. He is still in the business of communicating with His friends – if we have the ears to hear His voice. But friendship is two-way. A friendship will eventually die if the communication is only one-sided.

So let's start by communicating with Jesus and then ask Him to help us become more proficient at communicating with our friends and family.

# CHAPTER EIGHT

# MORE THAN CONQUERORS

I have learned to be content whatever the circumstances
. . . I can do everything through Him who gives me
strength. (Philippians 4:11,13)

*Materials:*

A small glass of pure lemon juice, and a glass of honey and lemon mixed together.

*Talk:*

What are some of the most common problems we struggle with? These may include sickness – yours or a member of the family, bad nights, shortage of money, difficult neighbours, loneliness, relationship difficulties, stress, tiredness, sexual problems.

Some of the problems that arise can be sorted out by taking some kind of action. But for many difficulties there are no easy answers, and we are left wondering how we are going to survive with the mounting stress and painful feelings.

When a problem has no immediate solution are we doomed to live with frustration, depression, or anxiety for the duration? Or is there something positive we could do about it?

Victor Frankl had the horrendous experience of being incarcerated in a Nazi concentration camp during the Second World War, and asked himself a similar question. His was a circumstance well beyond his control. There was nothing he could do to change it, but he came to the conclusion that even in those extreme circumstances man still had a choice of action. The verdict was that in such a place everything could be taken away but one thing – the last of human freedoms: to choose one's attitude in any given set of circumstances. It is this spiritual freedom – which cannot be taken away – which makes life meaningful and purposeful.[15]

St Paul was also made a prisoner and he too was unable to do anything to free himself from that harsh situation. But he was not consumed with bad feelings, which so often add an extra burden to our lives and sap our energies when we are experiencing difficulties.

### Reading: Philippians 4:11–13

Paul said that he had 'learned' to be content. He had learned to have a healthy attitude in the middle of suffering. This letter to the Philippians was written at the end of a life beset with hardships and difficulties. I imagine that Paul was describing a feeling which had developed gradually through the practice of choosing the right attitude. Probably it was difficult at first, but it most likely grew easier with every new problem and every positive choice.

### Activity:

First pass around the cup of undiluted lemon and then a cup of lemon and honey mixed. Ask the group to dip in a finger and taste both.

Anger leaves a bitter taste but if you try asking God to bless the person who has caused the anger you will find your anger is mixed with sweetness and the feelings are much less bitter. When you are facing a difficult situation, try thanking God that He can bring good out of evil, and has promised never to leave you nor forsake you. You will find you begin to feel more peaceful.

So if we want to be as content at the end of our lives as Paul was, let's start choosing the right attitude in our difficulties now!

## Materials:

Print out the following:
   Blocked Goal = Anger, frustration
   Uncertain Goal = Anxiety, fear
   Unreachable Goal = Sadness, despair, hopelessness
   Failed Goal = Guilt, shame
(Copy enough for each member of the group to have one.)

## Talk:

We all set goals for ourselves – whether consciously or unconsciously. They range from very grand ones to fairly minor ones. One young man may set himself the goal of performing for his country at the Olympic Games; another may just want to save enough money to buy himself a pair of trainers. Some of our goals are very personal and important to us, such as the longing to have a baby, or to be successful at a particular activity. Goals are motivated by our needs. Needs may be practical ones to do with food, clothing and housing, or personal ones for security, significance and self-worth. These needs have a tendency to gnaw away at us, causing us to set our hearts on what we hope will satisfy them.

Problems arise when our goals are not fulfilled in the way we would like them to be. Then we spiral into a mixture of bad feelings. We struggle with emotions like shame, anxiety, anger, impatience and sadness. (Hand around the sheets of paper.)

*Discussion:*

Who can identify a negative feeling with a goal which has either failed, been blocked, is uncertain or unreachable?

*Reading: Proverbs 13:12; Matthew 6:33*

Jesus is addressing a very common emotion – anxiety. Haven't we all suffered from it? The answer, He says, is one of priorities. What we set our hearts upon will make all the difference between living a peaceful, contented life and one full of bad feelings.

Although Jesus had to eat, drink, sleep and do all the normal things that we have to do to survive, these things were never His main preoccupation. His major concern was always His Father's will. In fact on one occasion when His disciples asked Him if He was hungry, He told them that His food was to do the will of Him who sent Him and to finish His work (John 4:34). So when Jesus said that we should seek God's Kingdom first, He wasn't saying that the other things that concern us are wrong or evil – they are just of secondary importance. One of the major causes for painful emotions is our tendency to set our hearts on goals which belong to time and not to eternity.

When we struggle with difficult feelings it is always worth examining our goals. If the root of our discomfort is an unfulfilled hope, then the answer is to change our focus.

(To end ask the group to name some Kingdom goals.)
   *Kingdom goals:*
   To grow in our faith
   To live lives that honour God
   **To be good witnesses to our neighbours**

To get to know Jesus better
To love God more
To love our families
To love our neighbours as ourselves.

## THEME – BECOMING TWO-DIMENSIONAL

**Materials:**

Picture of face in the snow.

**Reading: 2 Corinthians 6:3–4, 8–10**

**Talk:**

In this passage Paul is authenticating his ministry by listing his sufferings in the cause of Christ. When the reader is just beginning to feel overwhelmed by them, he suddenly changes his tone. By the time we get to 'as having nothing and yet possessing everything', you can almost hear the triumph in his voice. But then the reader is left with a question mark. How can we be poor and yet make many rich? How can we have nothing and yet possess everything? Paul sounds a little mad.

**Activity:**

Pass the snow picture around and ask the group what they can see. It is an aerial picture of a snow scene. If you look carefully you can see a face which looks like the face of Jesus emerging.

Paul was seeing life in two dimensions. The first dimension, which is the easiest to see and be aware of, was his life on earth with all its frustrations, hardships and sufferings. But gradually, the second dimension came into focus – out of the rather bleak landscape emerged the spiritual reality. Rather like in the picture we've just seen. It was true, he was poor and had

nothing. But it was also true that in a spiritual sense he was rich
beyond measure. When Paul began to see that second dimension his whole attitude changed.

We all experience difficulties at some time in our lives because
they are part and parcel of life on this earth. Someone has said
that trouble is not a sign of inadequacy, stupidity or inferiority,
but rather an inescapable part of life – proof that you are a
card-carrying member of the human race.[16] But like Paul,
Christians are two-dimensional people. Sometimes it is hard to
see that other dimension. We struggle to sense God's presence
when we are in the midst of problems, just as some of us have
struggled to see the face in the snow. But whether we sense it or
not, God is still there. And because He is there, we can experience the dimension of His Kingdom even while we are still
living here on earth. We too can be: 'Sorrowful, yet always

rejoicing; poor, yet making many rich; having nothing, and yet possessing everything' (2 Corinthians 6:10).

### Talk:

When we are in physical pain it is hard to forget it. Pain demands our attention. It takes no discipline at all to think about the part of our body which hurts. Similarly, if we have a difficult situation to contend with, it is on our minds most of the time. We don't have to force ourselves to think about it.

When physical pain or difficult circumstances carry on for any length of time we begin to wilt under the strain. The Bible is a very practical book and because so many of the characters in the Bible went through difficult times there is a lot in it to help us face our own problems. St Paul in particular gives us many tips for dealing with suffering.

### Reading: 2 Corinthians 4:18

Pain, difficulty, problems, cry out for attention. We don't have to discipline ourselves to focus on them. They do it for us. But we do have to discipline ourselves to focus on those things which do not demand our attention because they are unseen – the things which pertain to the Kingdom of God. In practical terms what does this mean? (Leave some time for suggestions.)

Some suggestions might include:
    The fact that God promises to be with us and never leave us.
      (Deuteronomy 31:6)

The fact that all things work for good in the end. (Romans 8:28)

The fact that Jesus left the Holy Spirit to help us. (John 14:17–18)

The fact that trials produce the good fruit of maturity in our lives. (James 1:2–4)

The fact that one day there will be no more pain, tears or death. (Revelation 21:4)

A man called Thomas Chalmers coined the expression: 'The expulsive power of a greater affection.' (Think up your own example or use the following.)

A woman may be afraid of flying, but when her only daughter and grandchildren go to live in Canada, she finds that her desire to see them is greater than her fear of flying. The greater affection for the daughter expelled the fear.

When we are experiencing stress or anxiety on account of temporary circumstances, at least in comparison to eternity, one of the antidotes is to meditate on the splendour of God's eternal Kingdom and the joy that awaits the believer. Certainly Paul was helped to cope with his sufferings in this way. In his letter to the Romans he says: 'I consider that our present sufferings are not worth comparing with the glory that will be revealed in us' (Romans 8:18).

## THEME – TRUSTING GOD

**Materials:**

Five mugs or cups.

**Talk:**

Sometimes we make the mistake of thinking that expressing negative feelings is unspiritual. The Bible speaks of 'self-control' as a fruit of the Spirit (Galatians 5:23). Yet it also tells us to be angry but not to sin (Ephesians 4:26). So self-control is not suppressing our feelings it is expressing them appropriately, in the right way and at the right time.

(Give your own example or use the following.) For example, if there is a very bad storm, with thunder and lightning, and you have a family of young children who are very frightened, you try to keep calm for their sakes. Once they have gone back to sleep then you can express your fear to your husband, or to God.

People in the Bible, from David and the prophets, through to Jesus and Paul, expressed their negative feelings in a very open way. One of the prophets in the Old Testament who expressed his anguish about the state of his nation was a man called Habakkuk.

**Reading: Habakkuk 1:2,3; 2:4**

Habakkuk was totally honest with God and did not hide his feelings. God wasn't angry with him for his negativity; instead

He tried to explain to Habbakkuk how He was going to use the ruthless Babylonians to deal with Israel's sin. During the course of this explanation it seems as if God realised that man is a finite being who can never fully grasp His infinite purposes. At this point He slipped in the key to Habakkuk's peace of mind, and the key for humankind's peace of mind down through the ages: 'But the righteous will live by his faith.' In other words, God told Habakkuk: 'My people (the righteous) just have to trust me.' In the most difficult circumstances, when nothing appears to make any sense to us, we have to trust that God can see the whole picture and will bring good out of evil in the end.

A good illustration of this is the example of a police helicopter. A police car arrives at the scene of a bank break-in just as the robbers are disappearing in the getaway car. They take off in pursuit, but the robbers are taking so many short cuts that the police soon lose them. But above them the police helicopter – the 'eye in the sky' – has spotted the robbers' car and relays the route it is taking to the police car below. The helicopter can see the whole picture and all the policemen on the ground can do is to trust them, and follow instructions from above.

In the same way God is like the 'eye in the sky'. He can see the whole picture, including our circumstances, from beginning to end. We only see a very small piece of the picture and all we can do is to trust Him. Trust that He knows best, loves us and will guide us perfectly. Job, the classic sufferer, once said: 'Though he slay me, yet will I hope in him' (Job 13:15).

*Activity:*

Set out the mugs across the floor. Ask for two volunteers. Blindfold the first volunteer and ask the other volunteer to guide her through the mugs safely.

God sees what we cannot possibly see. That's why we have to trust Him. 'Faith is not a bridge over troubled waters but a pathway through them' (Anon).

## THEME – A DECLARATION OF FAITH

*Materials:*

On a piece of cardboard make a notice which reads: 'Hallelujah Anyway!'

*Talk:*

Ask the group members the question: 'When you are in the middle of trouble what is the thing you most want to do?' (Give the group time to answer.) When we are going through a difficult time most of us want to share our problems with someone else. The old adage: 'A trouble shared is a trouble halved' is true. It is important for all of us to have people we can talk to when we are going through difficulties. It is also important for our peace of mind that we learn to trust God. But sometimes it is difficult.

Life is full of things we do not understand. It is unreal to pretend we don't ever have doubts in our minds, especially about the major theological problem of suffering. There are times when we are tempted to ask God why He allows certain things to happen. We will never find a completely satisfactory answer to such questions. God is infinite. We are finite. He is awesomely greater than we can ever imagine or think. For us to understand the mind of God would be like trying to explain the internet to an ant.

The prophet Habakkuk had a problem understanding why God allowed such bad things to happen. Instead of being angry at Habakkuk's complaint, God took the time to explain His plans to him, but the explanation was hard for the prophet to comprehend. God then challenged Habakkuk to trust Him. The following verses are a response to the challenge.

### Reading: Habakkuk 3:17–18

Habakkuk made a decision to trust God through thick and thin. This song of praise is his declaration of faith.

It is easy to say we trust God when things are going well, but not so easy when things go the other way. A demonstration of trust is when we praise God in the middle of trouble. Such praise tells God more than anything else that we not only believe in Him, but we also trust that His plans for us are ultimately for good and not evil.

The following rhyme was found on the wall of a concentration camp:

> I believe in the sun,
> Even when it is not shining.
> I believe in love,
> Even when I feel it not.
> I believe in God,
> Even when he is silent.[17]

It helps us to share our troubles with others, but learning to praise God despite our circumstances will, more than anything else, save us from sinking beneath the storms of life.

(Show the group the notice, 'Hallelujah Anyway!' Suggest they might all make one to put next to their kitchen sink.)

## THEME – THE POWER OF THANKSGIVING

*Talk:*

'A cheerful heart is good medicine' (Proverbs 17:22). We all feel better when we have had a good laugh. In fact some experts are investigating laughter for its clinical benefits. Apparently laughter releases endorphins and painkilling hormones.[18] A man called Norman Cousins wrote about his battle with an incurable and painful disease. Doctors gave him a 500 to one chance of recovery. Cousins decided to treat himself by eating healthy food and by undergoing laughter therapy! He booked himself into a hotel room with a pile of funny videos. He watched hours of 'Candid Camera', the Marx brothers and cartoons – anything that would make him laugh. He discovered that every time he had ten minutes of laughter he would have two hours free of pain. He eventually amazed the doctors by making a complete recovery.[19]

*Reading: 1 Thessalonians 5:16–18*

God knows what will do us good. However, it is hard to be joyful all the time, even if we are convinced of its therapeutic benefits. When the baby has been sick all night and our washing machine has gone wrong, when we have guests for dinner and the apple pie has burnt, when we have run out of housekeeping money and it's only Wednesday, then it's difficult to be joyful!

These verses tell us that it is God's will for us to be joyful and to give thanks in all circumstances. Is it possible to do this without hypocrisy?

## Discussion:

(Ask the group to discuss how they can obey this injunction without hypocrisy.)

Whatever we may be going through, God is still God and therefore worthy of our praise. Imagine if you had a terrible migraine headache and the Queen was due to visit your house that day. You would still do your best to welcome her and honour her, simply because she was the Queen. In the same way, however we feel, God has not changed – He is still the Creator of the whole universe and beyond. He holds it all together and without Him we would disintegrate into a thousand pieces. He is the sovereign King of kings – greater and more awesome than we can possibly imagine, and yet He loves us even more than we love our children. So surely such a God is worthy of our praise and thanks, even when the sun is not shining and life is difficult. He is always 'Our Father in Heaven'. He has never signed off!

## Activity:

Ask everyone to think of two things for which they can thank God and then share these with the person next to them.

# CHAPTER NINE
# KINGDOM PRACTICES

## The Christian Counter-Culture

## THEME – BEING SALT AND LIGHT

*Materials:*

One small packet of unsalted crisps and one packet of salted. A torch and a tea towel.

*Activity:*

Pass the crisps around and ask the group to try both packets and say which they like the best. Most will say the salty ones. Then ask the group what else salt is good for. (Cleansing, preserving.)

*Reading: Matthew 5:13–16*

*Talk:*

Have you ever wondered if your life has a purpose? It may be that looking after a family is your priority at present. Some of you may help in a community project. You may have a part-time job, or maybe you support and help in your local church. Whatever your occupation, wherever you live and work, God has set you there for a purpose. He wants you to permeate secular society and bring a good flavour to the lives of those around you. Also to preserve society from becoming corrupt and to be a cleansing agent when corruption is found.

Let's think what this might mean in practical terms. (Ask the group to make suggestions.) (Give an example from your own

162 77 BIBLE STUDIES FOR 21ST CENTURY MUMS

life, or of someone you have read about.) For example, in the
nineteenth century Lord Shaftesbury fought for the abolition
of child labour and William Wilberforce for the abolition of
slavery.

As well as being salt, Jesus said that His disciples were the
light of the world. It sounds a daunting task, and those hesi-
tant, uneducated fishermen must have wondered how on earth
so few could give light to the whole world. Jesus gave the illustration of a city set on a hill that cannot be hidden. During the
last world war enormous effort was put into blacking out the
cities. No light was to show during the hours of darkness,
because this would give the enemy a target for his bombing
raids. It was an almost impossible task, and the wardens were
constantly having to knock on doors warning people that there
was a light showing. Light is hard to hide.

It is hard to think of a city on a hill being hidden, and it is hard
to think of someone lighting a torch or candle and placing it
under a bowl. (Switch on the torch.) Light is supposed to light
up the darkness. What would be the point if it were switched on
and then covered? (Demonstrate with the tea towel.) It's ridiculous.

In the same way, if we are Christians and yet never stand up for
what is right, speak out about the injustice, or show mercy to
the poor and disenfranchised, what is the point of being here in
the world at all? In these days we are surrounded by suffering,
moral disintegration and spiritual darkness. By the way we live
our lives, even while doing the ordinary everyday tasks, we
should bring some light into our homes and communities. So
often we are scared of what people will think of us, and tempted
to hide our light. We fear ridicule if we stand out as different,
so we say nothing. In fact, we often try our best to blend into

the landscape. But that would be the same as placing the light under a bowl. Ridiculous! 'So let your light shine,' says Jesus, 'That people may see your good works and glorify your Father in Heaven!'

## THEME – GOING THE SECOND MILE

*Materials:*

Large mallet and small hammer.

*Activity:*

Someone hits you with a small hammer. Not satisfied with hitting them back with a small hammer, you look around for a large mallet. (Brandish the mallet.) That way, we think the offender will really learn a lesson.

*Talk:*

We have all watched small children at play. One child takes another's toy; the offended child quickly grabs the toy back and then uses the toy as a weapon to give the offender a quick whack on the head. It's human nature. Just like children, when we are hurt, we want our own back, though adults tend to be a little more subtle and surreptitious when they take revenge. We don't make it look too obvious. Nevertheless we long to make the person who has hurt us feel the same pain that we have felt. The problem with revenge is that we have a tendency to overdo it. It starts off with a desire for justice, but then we feel the person hasn't learned his lesson, or isn't sorry enough, so we hit a little harder. For this reason God gave the commandment: 'An eye for an eye and a tooth for a tooth.' It was for damage limitation.

*Reading: Matthew 5:38–41*

God set a limit for His people. Then Jesus came along and, while He reinforced God's law, He went a step further. He sug-

164

gested that if someone hits you, instead of hitting back, allow that person to hit you again; if someone wants to sue you, and take away your best coat, don't resist him, let him have your raincoat also. This sort of behaviour goes completely against the grain. But that is what it means to be people of the Kingdom. Society shakes its head in unbelief when it finds Christians being salt and light in a world where it's normal to hate, to take revenge, and to be unforgiving. So if someone is rude to you, maybe you could start by inviting her round for coffee.

Even more shocking was Jesus' talk about going the second mile. The Jews were under Roman rule at the time and it was the law that if a Roman soldier met a Jew he could compel him to carry his baggage for exactly a mile. Imagine how a poor farmer would feel, tired by his day's work in the fields, being made to carry a soldier's equipment for a mile. Despite the obvious injustice Jesus told his disciples not only to go the mile, but to keep going a little further.

I wonder what going the extra mile would mean for us? Ask the group to think of situations at home when they have done so, or could have but didn't.

Going the extra mile causes people to sit up and take notice. If there is someone in your family you would like to influence for Christ, go the extra mile and see if it doesn't say more to them than all your words. Remember, actions speak louder than words.

## Theme – Kingdom priorities

### Materials:

Leaflets from the local bank about pensions and savings schemes. A blackboard and chalk or flip chart and pen.

### Talk:

With almost every post we receive mail from banks and building societies trying to encourage us to join their various schemes. Mostly we throw them in the waste paper basket because we are either not in a position to save anything, or we already have a pension or savings plan. Whatever we do with such leaflets, we are, nevertheless, all concerned about money.

How many watch programmes on TV where people can win a lot of money or goods? Programmes such as 'Who Wants to be a Millionaire'. What is so interesting about them? (Short time of discussion.) Usually it is because we identify with the person playing the game and imagine what we would do if we were to win a million.

### Reading: Matthew 6:19–24

In this part of Jesus' sermon He was teaching about priorities. Money has a tendency to take up a lot of our attention. We either need to acquire some, spend some, or save some. Whichever it is, most families spend a great deal of time discussing it, thinking about it and even arguing about it. The fact is we cannot live without it, and life can be made a great deal easier and more comfortable when we have it. For these reasons there is a temptation to make it a high priority in our lives. Jesus warned His disciples not to let this happen. And there are some simple reasons for this:

1. Money and material possessions are uncertain and have a limited power. They have a tendency to come and go. The stock exchange could crash and all our savings could be lost overnight, or one day we could find ourselves or our spouse out of work and on a very limited income. If we are trusting in money to bring us happiness and to make us feel secure, then in a moment our world could be in ruins.

2. Another reason is that in terms of its value it is limited. Money lasts for only a lifetime and has no place in eternity. (Place a dot on the blackboard to represent time. Then underneath draw a line from one side of the board to the other to represent eternity.) Time is a mere dot, almost invisible, in comparison to eternity, which has no beginning and no ending. Logic should tell us that it would be wiser to invest in eternity.

3. Money commands our attention and therefore competes with our commitment to God. 'It is impossible,' says Jesus, 'to serve two masters.' We all know how hard it is to try and please everyone. When we try someone ends up being disappointed. Money has to be subservient to God. Loving God and loving others should be our primary focus. Money and possessions have to serve our first love and not become our master. Once the scales tip in the wrong direction and money begins to grow in significance and importance, then we will find our love for God will begin to grow cold.

*Materials:*

Buy or make a smart invitation to a formal dinner party.

*Discussion:*

What would be your first thought if you received an invitation like this? (Show the invitation.) Spend some time discussing the question.

*Talk:*

Most of us would immediately ask ourselves the question: 'Whatever shall I wear?' We would tend to spend the months or weeks between the invitation arriving and the actual event worrying about what to wear. We would probably ask friends for their opinion. We could change our minds several times and as the event drew nearer our anxiety level would rise every time we thought about it.

*Reading: Matthew 6:25–34*

Jesus knows us very well. He knows that we are inclined to worry about many things, particularly practical everyday issues. But worry is not a Kingdom activity. He faced His disciples with the truth about this common reaction to everyday problems. He told them that worry was a waste of time. No one can add a single hour to his life by worrying.

Worry is useless, unless it results in action that resolves the problem. We might lose a good night's sleep by worrying about

something, and in the morning all that has happened is that we
have exhausted ourselves. The problem has not changed one
iota. Worry is also a denial of God's care of us. Jesus drew
attention to the birds of the air and the flowers of the field.
They don't worry and God feeds them and clothes them. We are
more valuable to God than these, so surely we can believe God
will look after us. The bottom line is that worry is a failure to
trust God with the details of our lives. We are behaving just like
people who do not know and love Him, and spend their lives
chasing after material things.

We live in a stress-filled world. A recent survey said that an esti-
mated 302,000 people in Britain reported suffering from work-
related stress and a further 261,000 believed themselves to be
suffering from a 'stress-related' condition.[20] In such a society a
relevant testimony to God's love would be to remain peaceful
in the face of the stresses and strains of life. We can do this if
we consciously put the concerns of God's Kingdom first; then
the less important issues will pale in significance.

You may well be saying to yourselves: 'Well, that's fine when the
worry is as trivial as the clothes you wear. But what about the big
concerns, such as losing a job and not being able to pay the mort-
gage?' The principle remains the same. Worry is still a waste of
time. To be concerned about our family's wellbeing is natural,
but worry achieves nothing. It doesn't earn one penny more. It
usually doesn't resolve the problem. It doesn't clothe the family.
It just drains our energy and makes us unhappy. Seeking God in
the situation would be more fruitful.

# THEME – DON'T JUDGE

## Materials:

Some Weight Watchers diet sheets. A list of low-fat foods (enough copies for everyone to have one). A cream bun.

Tell the group that today the subject is dieting. Hand the sheets and the list around. Tell them you want them to study these so that they will be aware of what foods they need to eat to lose weight. Then while they are looking at the leaflets take out the cream bun and take a bite! Discuss their reactions to what you have just done.

## Talk:

What a hypocrite I would be if I had the nerve to lecture you on dieting, while I was eating all the wrong foods myself.

## Reading: Matthew 7:1–5

Jesus paints a humorous picture of someone trying to help another person get some grit out of his eye, while he is blinded by a huge plank sticking out of his own eye. Hypocrisy is being blind to our own faults, but highly critical of other people's shortcomings. Jesus is very specific that judging others is not a Kingdom activity, even though many Christians spend time doing it.

Jesus is the ultimate model for our lives. So it is worth noticing how He reacted to people with glaring faults. One day some religious people presented Him with a woman who had been caught in the act of adultery. The law demanded that the woman be punished. They wanted to wrong-foot Jesus so they asked Him what He would do. For a while Jesus just doodled in the sand. When they kept on questioning Him He straightened up and said to them: 'If any one of you is without sin, let him be the first to throw a stone at her' (John 8:7). Then He bent down and continued with His doodling. One by one the disconcerted men slunk away. Then Jesus said to the woman: 'Has no one condemned you? Then neither do I condemn you. Go now and leave your life of sin.' Jesus didn't condemn her, but neither did He condone her lifestyle.

We are so often like the religious leaders of Jesus' day: quick to judge others for their shortcomings, as if we ourselves were blameless. So how can we change this tendency? (Ask the group for some ideas.)

*Suggestions*

1. Tell ourselves that we have to be imitators of Jesus. Jesus did not come to judge the world but to save it.
2. Remind ourselves that we are not blameless. We could even make a checklist of the 'planks' we should be attempting to remove from our own lives.
3. Adopt the attitude of a servant instead of a judge. We are called to serve one another, which means we should come alongside someone in difficulties and try and help them, instead of standing in judgement over them.
4. Pray that God will open our eyes to the truth about ourselves, and infuse us with compassion for others, especially those in difficulties. Remember, 'Mercy triumphs over judgment!'(James 2:13).

## Materials:

List of Christmas requests from several four- or five-year-olds. Buy or make some of your favourite biscuits. Place them in the centre of the group, but keep them covered with a cloth.

## Talk:

We all have experience of these lists. (Read out the list of children's Christmas requests.) Perhaps we can remember writing one ourselves, many years ago! Most children trust that whoever reads their lists – Santa or their parents – will give them what they most desire for Christmas. Few parents can resist their child's implicit trust in the generosity of the adult world around them. Even when money is in short supply, they will go without themselves to see their children have what they have requested, within reason. Within reason! No caring and wise parent is likely to give a child they love an unsuitable present. For example, a pet is often found on a child's list of requests. But if that child is allergic to animal fur, no mother will risk giving her a pet. Or a sixteen-year-old is hoping for a car on his next birthday when he will be eligible to learn to drive. Would a loving father give that young man a fast and powerful sports model for his first car? However, within limits, most parents do their best to fulfil their children's wishes.

## Reading: Matthew 7:7–12

In this passage Jesus encouraged His disciples to ask God their Father for what they need. It is interesting to note that Jesus does not say that they will get exactly what they have asked for, only that they will receive. God hears and answers our prayers, but like any good parent He doesn't always give us what we think we want or need exactly when we think we must have it. Nor would He give us something that would harm us and therefore, though He always answers our prayers, it is not always in the way we expect.

It would seem that effective prayer has certain aspects to it. The first is persistence. Ask (or beg), seek and knock. These three words give a distinct impression of stubborn determination. Effective prayer does not give up. Hudson Taylor was a famous missionary in the early part of the last century. Before he left for China he said that he wanted to learn *to move men, through God, by prayer alone.*[21] He was a man who gave himself to prayer all his life and saw many people touched by God through his prayers. God is looking for people who have this sort of resolute attitude.

Another aspect of prayer is trust; trust that God knows best. Our prayers are not always answered in the way we want and without faith in God's goodness it would be tempting to give up. Another famous Christian in the nineteenth century was a man called Billy Bray. He was a humble Cornish miner who was saved by Jesus from a life of drunkenness and debauchery. He was a man of great faith and when something happened which he didn't exactly understand he would exclaim: 'Well, Father do know best.' In his simplicity Billy trusted that God had his best interests at heart.[22]

Jesus ended this little bit of his teaching with what is commonly known as 'the Golden Rule' – 'Do to others what you would have them do to you.' He had been talking about God's love and generosity. Then He went on to encourage His hearers to be generous too. So I have brought some of my favourite biscuits to share!

*Activity:*

Hand around the plate of biscuits.

## THEME – LAYING FOUNDATIONS

*Materials:*

Early Learning books on the three 'Rs', and a children's Bible.

*Talk:*

Foundations are important. If any of you have ever watched a house being built from the beginning you will see the foundations being put in first. The foundations determine the size of the building. If it is to be a high rise building then the foundations need to be even deeper than for a normal two-storied house. The safety of a building can be endangered when builders take shortcuts in their work. A house has to withstand a lot of wear and tear – especially from the weather. The foundations determine how well the building stands the strain.

*Reading: Matthew 7:24–29*

Jesus likened the man who heard His words and put them into practice to a man who had built his house upon the rock. When the storm came his house didn't collapse because he had built it on a solid foundation. The man who built his house on sand was like the man who heard the words of Jesus but took no notice. Building a house on sand is not a wise move! During the difficult times it is unlikely to survive. However, the shortcut mentality is very common. It is easy to read the story and think how stupid the man was, but the truth is we all have a tendency to look for shortcuts in life. Most of us know what we think would be the best way to live our lives. We may have had some early Christian teaching, or had good input from our parents. But we all have a bias towards doing what comes naturally, easily, and would give us the most pleasure.

For example, most parents would say that they desire to build good foundations into their children's lives.

Discuss what these foundations would be (time allowing).

*Talk:*

We need to start teaching the difference between right and wrong from an early age so that our children have a moral foundation to their lives. We need to pray with them and talk to them about God's love so that early on their spiritual lives will start developing. (Show the Bible.) As soon as they are ready we ought to help them conquer the three 'Rs', upon which the rest of their education will be built. (Show the books.) But life is busy. There is never enough time during the day to do all we would like to do. In the hectic rush we take the easy route and put off until tomorrow what we should be doing today. Sadly it is hard to put in those important foundations later. In a person, as with a building, they have to go in early on.

It isn't enough just to agree with the teachings of Jesus. We have to make the effort to practice them. So when Jesus says: 'Love your neighbour', or 'Forgive those who hurt you' we must do more than nod in agreement. We have to actually do it. By obeying His commands we gain moral and spiritual strength. At times life can be difficult. But when the storms rage around us, we will find a strength within ourselves to rise above the difficulties.

## CHAPTER TEN

# TRUE MATURITY

When I was a child, I talked like a child, I thought like a child, I reasoned like a child. When I became a man, I put childish ways behind me. (1 Corinthians 13:11)

## THEME – WHAT IS MATURITY?

*Materials:*

An instant camera if available (or an ordinary one).

*Talk:*

Babies are gorgeous. Toddlers are enchanting, especially when they are tucked up in bed, clean and peaceful! But would you feel the same about them if they stayed that way and never grew up? Imagine how we would react if they remained mentally, physically and emotionally immature.

God feels the same way about us. He wants us to grow up. When children mature they move from one developmental stage to another until they are fully adult. However, even if they have adult bodies, this doesn't mean they will be mature in every other way. To be fully mature we need to be socially, mentally, physically, emotionally and spiritually developed.

What does true maturity look like?

*Reading: Ephesians 4:11–13, Romans 8:29*

God's will is that we are being transformed into the likeness of Jesus. Only then will we be mature and grown-up in every way.

So if true maturity reflects Jesus, how can we reach such heights? (Open the question up for discussion.)

There are many things we can do to help us become more like Jesus. One of the most effective disciplines is to keep company with Him, and to look at Him often. When couples have spent many years together they develop similar mannerisms, tastes, and ways of thinking and behaving. One starts to tell a story and the other finishes it. They intuitively know what the other is going to say, before they have said it.

When a baby spends hours, days and months gazing up into the same adoring face, eventually a picture of the mother is imprinted, indelibly on the baby's mind and heart. So after a year or so the mother can leave the baby alone and that baby won't panic, because he carries a picture of mummy around in his subconscious. This process is called 'internalisation'. It's a bit like the way a camera works.

(Show the camera and take a photo of all or a part of the group.) I focus the camera on the group, squeeze the button which opens the shutter, allowing the light to imprint the image of the group on the film.

(If it is an instant camera, let the group see the end result.)

The more we read and think about Jesus and allow the light of His presence to flood into our lives, the more likely we are to grow up into His image.

## THEME – PHYSICAL MATURITY

*Material:*

A potted plant in full bloom.

*Talk:*

In our quest for maturity we have to look at it from every angle, even from the physical aspect. We know that normally people reach physical maturity by the age of eighteen years, so we often presume that this is automatic and not something about which we have to be too concerned.

Look at this plant. It is fully developed, but to reach this state of maturity it has received lots of care in the shape of water, light, feeding and dead heading, and will continue to need this care if it is to live out its full lifespan. We may be physically mature now but to sustain ourselves we need the same sort of care and attention.

To maintain good health we need:
1. *Understanding.* Knowing what our bodies need in the way of exercise, healthy diet, sun, and rest.
2. *Discipline.* Eating the right foods and getting enough exercise takes effort. There is a lot to tempt us into bad habits.
3. *Persistence.* Putting in an effort just once in a while is not enough. We have to continue to be disciplined.

Someone once defined discipline as the choice of achieving what you really want by doing things you don't really want to do. After doing this successfully for some time, discipline becomes the choice of achieving what you really want by doing things you now want to do! In other words, we can become disciplined and enjoy it – after years of practising.[23]

## Discussion:

Why is it important for us to keep our bodies healthy?

There are many reasons. But one we don't always think about comes in our reading.

## Reading: 1 Corinthians 6:19

We are told to honour God with our bodies, because they are the temple of the Holy Spirit. If God's Spirit dwells within us then it is our job to keep His house in good order.

Jesus had to grow up, just like us. Isaiah prophesied that Jesus would grow up like a tender shoot (Isaiah 53:2). After His baptism in the River Jordan, being full of the Holy Spirit He was led by the Spirit into the desert for forty days, where He fasted. When He began his public ministry He was fully grown and able to withstand the temptations Satan put in His way, because He was full of the Spirit, disciplined and mature in every way.

*Materials:*

A riddle or mental puzzle. For example, a knight and a maiden were walking through the woods and entered a large clearing. In the middle of the clearing were a number of goats and a number of unicorns playing about. The maiden remarked that she saw a total of forty-four horns. The knight replied that there were twice as many unicorns as goats. How many unicorns and how many goats were there? Answer is: eleven goats and twenty-two unicorns.)

*Activity:*

Read out your own riddle, or the example given, and ask the group if they can give the correct answer.

*Talk:*

Many of us presume that mental maturity is being able to answer difficult questions, to have a PhD, or at least a university degree. But what does the Bible say about it?

*Reading: Luke 2:40, Matthew 13:54*

Mental maturity is about having wisdom. People asked where Jesus got His wisdom, not which university He went to. We can have much learning, have the brains to solve the most difficult problems, but have very little wisdom.

*Discussion:*

How would you describe wisdom?

1. Wisdom is about making sensible decisions based on good information. Often we make decisions based on facts, which we then mix with some hidden agenda of our own. (Give a personal example or use the following.) For example, imagine a young mother who wants to send her child to playschool. There is a very good one near her house. She has all the information about it and knows that it has a good reputation and is within her price range. But she decides against it. The reason is that she has a hidden motive for avoiding that school. She knows that, at a time when she was a rebellious teenager, one of the leaders used to be a neighbour, and she was once very rude to her. Now she is embarrassed to meet her again.

   Wisdom would lead the young mother to resolve the situation. The wisest thing would be to see the teacher, apologise for her bad behaviour, show her that she has changed and then send her child to that school.

2. Wisdom is also about being flexible, willing to change and being open to new ideas. We can become mentally stuck in a rut. We think there is only one way to do things – our way!

3. Being willing to learn is also a mark of wisdom. Mental maturity means having a teachable spirit – ready to listen and learn from others.

'But the wisdom that comes from heaven is first of all pure; then peace-loving, considerate, submissive, full of mercy and good fruit, impartial and sincere' (James 3:17).

## THEME – SOCIAL MATURITY

*Materials:*

An imitation rose sprayed with perfume. A bunch of real flowers. A *Hello* magazine, or one that has pictures of the rich and famous.

*Talk:*

It would be easy to regard these people as socially mature (show the pictures in the magazine) because they are admired, popular and accepted into top society. Or we may think that living up to other people's standards, pleasing others and never having any conflict is being socially mature.

*Reading: Matthew 9:11*

Jesus was not governed by other people's standards. In fact He shocked many of the religious leaders of the day. He was never controlled, either by other people's opinions or their expectations of Him.

*Discussion:*

So how would you describe social maturity?

1. Social maturity is being at home with other people, even when they have different ideas from your own. It is being able to listen patiently to another person's point of view, even when you don't agree with them.
2. Social maturity is being able to give as well as receive gifts or

compliments from other people. Many of us are very good at giving to others but not good at receiving.

3. Social maturity is being real with other people – not hiding behind a mask, and living in pretence. It's hard to be friends with people who are afraid to tell you who they really are.

To have someone love you 'warts and all' is a wonderful gift. To have someone love a 'pseudo' self one is projecting for effect is a source of great stress. And in the end our friends will discover the truth, and what then?

It's much like this rose. It smells like a real rose. It looks like a real rose. But in fact it is only an imitation. (Pass round the imitation rose.) Most people would much rather be given a bunch of roses straight from the garden – thorns and all!

(Pass around the real flowers.)

## THEME – EMOTIONAL MATURITY

*Materials:*

A mirror.

*Talk:*

A truly mature person should be mature in every way and particularly in the area of the emotions. Most of us were brought up to be afraid of strong feelings. We live with the misconception that the most appropriate way of handling our feelings is to suppress them. We are dubious about expressing them, however appropriately.

*Reading: John 11:35* is the shortest verse in the Bible, but shows us that Jesus was not afraid of expressing His feelings of grief.

Mark 11:15–17 When Jesus saw what was happening in His Father's house He did not hide His anger. He showed His feelings in no uncertain terms.

*Discussion:*

After reading these verses how would you describe emotional maturity?

Sum up what has been said and add these items if they have not already been expressed:

1. Emotional maturity is understanding that a feeling is a response to a thought or an experience.

2. Emotional maturity is accepting that all our feelings are unique gifts of God. 'Your heart . . . is the wellspring of life' (Proverbs 4:23).
3. Emotional maturity is being able to name our feelings – both the good and bad, and to own them instead of blaming others.

John Powell, an American university lecturer and writer, used to have this notice stuck to his mirror over the sink: 'You are looking at the face of the person who is responsible for your happiness.'[24]

We are responsible for our feelings and no one else. Immaturity wants to blame someone else for them. Someone else may have been the cause of the feelings, but they are nevertheless our feelings and only we can decide what we are going to do about them.

### Activity:

(Pass round the mirror and encourage everyone to take a look at themselves.) The person you see staring back at you is the one responsible for your happiness today.

4. Emotional maturity is also learning to express our feelings in an appropriate manner. It is what one does with one's feelings that decides emotional maturity.

Sin occurs when we express our feelings inappropriately, and sickness may occur when we suppress them inappropriately.

*Discussion:*

How would you describe someone who is spiritually mature?

*Talk:*

We sometimes equate spiritual maturity with super-spirituality. We look up to those who pray a lot, are always reading their Bibles, fast often, have heavenly visions, give prophetic words and exercise all the spiritual gifts. We may put these sort of people on pedestals and think of them as super-spiritual. Though spiritually mature people may do all these things, doing them does not necessarily make you mature.

In his letter to the Colossians, Paul warns his readers not to be taken in by people who delight in false humility and the worship of angels. Such a person, he writes, goes into great detail about what he has seen and his unspiritual mind puffs him up with idle notions (Colossians 2:18).

People who try and place themselves in a category above other Christians are usually insecure and looking for a way of giving themselves some significance in the church. One church leader wrote: 'Over the years I have seen superspiritual Christians serve as leaders, lead worship and participate in every area of church life. I must say they are usually the most disruptive people a church can have . . . They can divide a church as fast as one can peel a banana.'[25] Such people will often use very

spiritual language and have rather condemning prophecies for
church leaders. Their spiritual language puts them above other
Christians, even though their personal lives may be a mess.

Jesus was a spiritually mature person. What marked Him out
as different from the other religious leaders of His day? Not His
'religiosity'. It was His obedience to His Father's will.

**Reading: John 4:34, Matthew 7:21**

Spiritual maturity is:

1.  Knowing God
2.  Becoming like Jesus
3.  Loving others as you love yourself
4.  But above all it is learning to do the will of God.

'There are only two kinds of people in the end. Those who say
to God: "thy will be done" and those to whom God says, in the
end, "thy will be done".'[26]

## THEME – THE BUMPY RIDE

*Materials:*

Enough copies of the wheel for each member of the group.

*Talk:*

For a few weeks we have been looking at true maturity. No one grows up overnight. Our children move imperceptibly from one stage of development to another. Those who are with them every day barely notice the difference. Only as we compare photos from last year can we see the change. All parents know that 'growing up' just happens. But it also needs a helping hand from them if it is to be accomplished successfully.

Good food leads to physical health – so we feed them well. Education will assist them to find employment one day – so we send them to school. Learning to share with other children enables them to form good relationships – so we teach them to be unselfish. Controlling strong emotions will avoid unnecessary disaster – so we help them express their feelings appropriately. The fear of God is the beginning of wisdom – so we pray with them and talk to them about God.

All the elements mentioned have to be ongoing to be effective. Parents start the ball rolling but our children have to keep it rolling once they are adults, taking responsibility for their own growth and maturity.

### Reading: Philippians 2:12

The word 'salvation' in this verse comes from the Greek word 'sozo', which means 'wholeness'. Therefore, as well as working out the meaning of our salvation in our everyday lives, this verse also gives us the idea that we should be working at becoming whole, while God works in us and with us.

It may seem harder work for some than others. For example, many of us were given very little help by our parents in handling difficult feelings. Consequently we run from conflict, don't know how to grieve for our losses, and remain fearful of showing even our positive feelings to others. There is an imbalance in our lives and this may be why we are experiencing a bumpy ride in life today. If this is true then we need to 'work at' wholeness in our lives. If we continue with stunted development in certain areas then we will likely pass this on to our children and they in their turn will experience a bumpy ride.

### Activity:

(Hand a picture of the wheel to each member of the group.) Imagine that the middle of the wheel is zero maturity. The spokes each signify an aspect of your life. The rim of the wheel signifies complete maturity. Now place a dot on the different spokes where you think you are right now in your journey towards maturity. So, for example, if you feel in good shape physically and know that you are doing your best to keep your body healthy, then place the dot towards the outer edge of the wheel. When you have placed all the dots, join them together to form an inner wheel.

### Talk:

What shape is your wheel? How rounded is it? An uneven wheel will give you a bumpy ride. The answer is to work on those weak areas of your life. One idea may be to ask for help from a friend, or from a more mature Christian.[27]

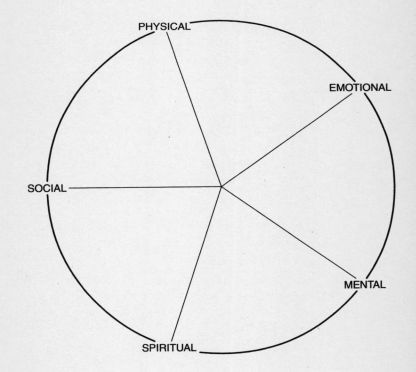

## CHAPTER ELEVEN

# SOME MEALTIMES IN THE BIBLE

Blessed are those who are invited to the wedding supper of the Lamb. (Revelation 19:9)

## THEME – THE IMPORTANCE OF FAMILY MEALS

### *Discussion:*

Ask the group why they think it is important to serve coffee or tea at these meetings. Suggestions: a sign of hospitality, gives opportunity to talk to people, relaxes people.

### *Talk:*

One or two might arrive gasping for a cup of tea or coffee, but most of us take a cup because of the reasons that have been given. In other words, a cup of coffee is not offered simply because of its ability to quench thirst and revive us. There is a lot more meaning behind the activity than the superficial act of drinking.

Families are finding it increasingly difficult to eat their meals together. We live in a frenetic world, where differing timetables, microwave meals, take-aways and TV have all combined to make family meals difficult to plan. Even the traditional Sunday roast is becoming a thing of the past. We have begun to treat meals as if they were just for the purpose of satisfying our hunger and nothing more. We forget that there is a lot more to mealtimes than just food.

For example:

1.  A meal eaten together strengthens family ties. One of the missing ingredients in modern society is a sense of belonging.

Family life is disintegrating and children are looking else-where for a place to belong. When we eat a meal together those ties are strengthened.

2. Sunday lunch has traditionally been a celebration meal. Families need times to celebrate their togetherness. It doesn't have to be done on a Sunday. It may be a Friday evening at the end of a busy week. Celebrations are times the children can remember with pleasure once they have grown up and flown the nest.

3. One of the main reasons for emotional breakdown is the lack of opportunity to share our anxieties and disappoint-ments, as well as our joys and successes, with those close to us. Mealtimes are opportunities to communicate. We all have a need to share with others near to us, not just superfi-cially but in depth. Let's not forget the old adage: 'The family that feels together heals together.' If yours is a Christian family then a mealtime also gives the opportunity to pray together, however briefly. Another appropriate saying is: 'The family that prays together stays together.'

The Bible is full of descriptions of banquets, feasts and simple meals, all enjoyed in fellowship with other people. Many won-derful things happened as people shared their food. In fact Jesus describes the fellowship He longs to enjoy with us in terms of eating together, because sharing a meal with someone offers the most opportunity for in-depth communication.

*Reading: Revelation 3:20*

## Theme – A thanksgiving meal

### *Materials:*

A plate of mince pies and some unleavened bread (bread with no raising agent, e.g. pitta bread). (Hand the mince pies round and ask the group what they remind them of.)

### *Talk:*

Every year we remember and celebrate the birth of Jesus Christ, and we do it in many different ways. We sing carols, we give presents, we prepare special foods like these mince pies and then we enjoy a celebration meal with our family. Although it is a Christian festival, in the midst of the busyness many of us barely give Jesus a thought. We may thank others for the presents we have been given but sometimes forget to thank God for the gift of His Son. (Hand round the unleavened bread and ask the group what it makes them think of.)

### *Reading: Exodus 12:1–11*

Since the time of the first Passover meal the Jews have celebrated it continuously in remembrance of their great deliverance from slavery in Egypt. The Passover meal is a time when Jewish families gather together and the head of the house leads them in a traditional act of thanksgiving.

Paul encourages us to overflow with thanksgiving (Colossians 2:7). God has given us so much to be thankful for. We have material things like food, shelter, and clothes, as well as families and friends from whom we receive love and to whom we can give love. We have a God who loves us and has promised never to leave us nor forsake us. We have a lot to be thankful for.

Jesus made a habit of being thankful. A mealtime is a good opportunity to remember to be grateful, not just for the food but for all God's goodness. It seemed that Jesus gave thanks whenever He had a meal. When He fed the five thousand He first looked up to heaven and gave thanks (Matthew 14:19). It was the same when He fed the four thousand. At the last supper in the upper room He took the cup of wine and gave thanks before giving it to the disciples. He took the bread and gave thanks before breaking it and handing it round to be eaten.

Just as we occasionally have to remind our children to say thank you, sometimes we need a reminder to give God thanks. Perhaps we could use mealtimes to jog our memories.

## THEME – A WEDDING FEAST

### Talk:

Every wedding day has its hair-raising moments. Encourage the group to share their experiences.

Wedding days have their difficult moments, but the problems don't end there. Every marriage has its difficulties too. In the beginning it can be quite hard to share our lives with another human being, even though we have chosen to do so. After years of being on one's own and making decisions without having to take others into account, being catapulted into a situation where you must explain your every move can be very difficult. Once that hurdle has been cleared and life has begun to get easier, children come along and a whole new set of problems arises – and so it goes on throughout our married lives. In fact it would be true to say that every marriage needs a miracle.

### Reading: John 2:1–11

At this wedding Jesus turned a difficulty into a blessing, but for it to happen the servants had to do exactly as Jesus told them. If we want our problems to be turned around then it's important that we take Jesus seriously and involve Him in our lives.

Another interesting part of the miracle was that the best was kept till last. At a celebration it was usual to serve the best wine first and keep the not so good for the end, because after a few drinks most people wouldn't notice that what they were drinking was second rate. But Jesus kept the best till last. For couples who stick at it, and try to do it the Jesus way, their testimony is that it gets better. In fact many would say 'the best was kept till last'. In these days, when marriages are under such strain, this has to be a miracle! But in God's economy He specialises in this sort of miracle.

The story is told of a lady in the US who had been told by her doctor that she was terminally ill. She called in her pastor and made arrangements for her funeral. Having chosen the hymns and readings, she surprised the pastor by making one last request: 'I want to be buried with a fork in my right hand.' The pastor was very surprised. So the woman explained. 'In all my years of attending church socials and potluck dinners, I always remember that when the dishes of the main course were being cleared, someone would inevitably lean over and say, "Keep your fork." It was my favourite part because I knew that something better was coming . . . like velvety chocolate cake or deep-dish apple pie. Something wonderful, and with substance! So, I just want people to see me there in that casket with a fork in my hand and I want them to wonder, "What's with the fork?" Then I want you to tell them: "Keep the fork . . . the best is yet to come."'[28]

However good or however bad is our experience of life, Jesus ensures that the best is yet to come.

## THEME – AN INTERRUPTED MEAL

### Materials:

A scented candle, a bottle of scent.

### Talk:

(Light the candle and allow the aroma to fill the room.) Most of us use scent occasionally. We usually keep the most expensive for very special occasions and keep the bottle away from our children because we don't want little fingers accidentally spilling precious perfume.

Jesus once had an encounter with some very expensive scent.

### Reading: John 12:1–5

Lazarus, Martha and Mary were friends of Jesus who lived in a place called Bethany, near to Jerusalem. The family had reason to be very grateful to Jesus, who had previously raised Lazarus from the dead in a very spectacular manner. Jesus often stayed in their house. On this occasion Jesus was in the middle of dinner with the family when Mary interrupted with an act of extravagant gratitude. She desperately wanted to show her love and thanks and the most expensive thing she had in the house was a jar of nard, so she poured a whole pint of this expensive scented oil over Jesus' feet, and then wiped His feet with her hair. Judas Iscariot was quick to point out that it was worth a whole year's wages. In today's terms this would be at least £10,000 or £15,000 ($15,000 to $23,000).

Some may have seen this act as an unnecessary interruption. Others may have seen it as embarrassingly emotional. Jesus saw it as a preparation for His burial. He saw the love and gratitude in Mary's heart, which had to overflow in some way. Judas saw the act as an unnecessary waste, but Jesus saw it as an act of extravagant worship. Then again, others may have wondered at Mary's loss of dignity. What she did was the work of a servant. Mary was a hostess, not a servant, but she forgot her position in her desire to pour out an offering to Jesus. She took a humble place at His feet. Others may have gasped with surprise, but Jesus loved her act of humility.

Jesus inevitably surprised people with His, apparently upside-down view of life. A few days after this event He knelt in the same humble position and washed His disciples' feet.

Mary had good reason to be grateful to Jesus because He had restored her brother to the family. But don't we too have reason to be grateful? Hasn't Jesus restored us and given us life? I wonder how prepared we are to be extravagant, emotional, and undignified sometimes in our gratitude to Him?

## THEME – GOD'S PROVISION

**Materials:**

Some ice cream wafers, a pot of honey and a knife.

**Talk:**

One of the names for God in the Bible is Yahweh-Jireh (the Lord will provide). Down through history, in instance after instance, God has provided for His people in miraculous ways. When they were crossing the desert, escaping from the Egyptians, they began to grumble and wish they were back in Egypt eating luxurious food. God graciously provided food for them. It was not a luxury food but it sustained them for forty years. They called the food manna or 'what is it'. It tasted a little like wafers and honey. (Pass round some wafers spread with honey.)

**Reading: Exodus 16:1–5, 31**

When the disciples asked Jesus to teach them to pray He taught them to ask God for their daily bread: 'Give us this day our daily bread.' Maybe Jesus was remembering the time in the wilderness when they were literally dependent on God for sustenance every day. In our Western world we rarely have to pray for our daily bread. We may not eat expensive food, but there is normally something in the cupboard or fridge to eat. So when we pray the Lord's Prayer, are we repeating meaningless words?

**Discussion:**

Allow the group some time to share their thoughts on this prayer.

The words 'daily bread' could be interpreted in two ways. Give us today tomorrow's bread, or give us today our needed bread (necessities). Some theologians think that asking God for tomorrow's bread means asking that we might today have a taster of God's supernatural sustenance, which one day, in His Kingdom, we will enjoy to the full.

What could this mean for us? (Healing, guidance, strengthening, etc.)

Certainly as citizens of God's Kingdom we can ask to be fed with supernatural sustenance from Heaven, but at the same time we are still human beings with physical needs. This prayer also encourages us to bring those needs to God. We may not literally have a need for bread, but we do have other necessities. Some of us might enjoy a few luxuries occasionally, and God is often good enough to provide them, but they are bonuses, which would hardly come under the heading of 'daily bread'.

Ask the group what they would class as necessities.

## THEME – A BREAKFAST TO REMEMBER

### Materials:

One messy, spoiled exercise book and one new one.

### Talk:

Do you remember the excitement of starting a new exercise book at school and the disappointment of spoiling it with ink blots, crossings out, and untidy work, then the joy of getting a new book and having the opportunity of starting all over again? (Show the two books.)

God is constantly giving us brand new starts. We blot our copy-book and when we tell Him about it He gives us a new one, so that we can begin again.

### Reading: John 21:4,10–17

After His crucifixion Jesus appeared to His disciples on several occasions. This story is one of those appearances. Not knowing what else to do, the disciples had returned to fishing. In the morning they returned to shore and Jesus was waiting for them with their breakfast already cooking. There is nothing nicer than a barbecue on the beach. But this was a specially memorable one.

Peter had boasted that he would never let Jesus down, but in the confusion and fear of Jesus' arrest he had three times denied knowing Him. The big fisherman cried with shame when he realised what he had done. It must have seemed like the end for him. On this morning the once proud Galilean was brought face to face with Jesus again. I expect he thought that Jesus would reprimand him. But instead Jesus asked him twice: 'Peter do you truly love me?' The word Jesus used here was one which meant do you love me with your whole personality, including your will, and Peter answered in the affirmative using the same word. The third time Jesus asked: 'Peter do you love me?' meaning spontaneously from the heart, and again Peter answered using the same words. Peter had denied Jesus three times, but in that exchange Jesus gave him the opportunity to reaffirm his devotion, and then reinstated him to care for His church.

Failure is painful. But much good can come out of failure. Peter had been too sure of himself – sure he would never fail – others yes, but him, never! Yet within a short time of this public boast he had let Jesus down abysmally. Peter did not really know himself until that moment of failure. He was unlikely to make such a public declaration again. Integrity and sincerity are born out of self-awareness. Once Peter had been made aware of his weakness he was in a position for God to use him. Humility took the place of pride, dependence took the place of self-reliance and a leader was born.

It was an unforgettable breakfast for Peter.

## THEME – THE WEDDING SUPPER OF THE LAMB

### Materials:

A big wedding hat. One large wedding invitation.

### Talk:

Everyone loves weddings. The biggest problem for the guests is what to wear. We can even lose sleep over it. Of course the bigger the hat the better, even if it obscures everyone else's view!

The bride usually looks back on the day with some regret because she didn't have time to enjoy it to the full. There was so much to think of and so many people to talk to and before she could really savour it all, the day was over, and all she was left with was an album of photos. Sometimes there are regrets about the service. Perhaps the choir was rather aged and squeaky! Or no one knew the hymns very well. There may be regrets about the actual day, but there may be more regrets about the marriage itself. Perhaps it has not turned out to be the fairy story one hoped for. We all long for a 'happy ever after' romance, but few relationships turn out to be so idyllic. We live in a real world, where we are assailed with problems and difficulties. Nothing seems to turn out exactly as we hoped.

The wedding day we may have enjoyed here on earth is fortunately not our last chance at a perfect union.

*Reading: Revelation 19:5–9*

One day there will be a wonderful wedding supper given in honour of Jesus, the Lamb of God, and His bride, the church. There will be no worries about what to wear because fine linen will be given her to wear. Those who are invited to that feast will be completely happy, blessed people. There will be no regrets at this wedding. It will more than likely go on for a very long time, and the music will be overwhelming. In fact the choir will be a multitude and their voices will sound like the roar of rushing waters and like loud peals of thunder as they shout: 'Hallelujah!'

There will never have been or ever will be a wedding celebration like it. The great news is that we are all invited to be present. Our invitation has already been sent. Not only are we invited to be present but we are actually invited to be the main participant along with the bridegroom. Every believer is part of the church of Christ, and Paul likens the church to the bride of Christ. All we have to do is to say 'yes' to the invitation (show the invitation card).

# NOTES

1 Neil Anderson, *Victory Over the Darkness*, Monarch, 1992, p.65

2 Florence Littauer, *Raising the Curtain on Raising Children*, Word Pub., Milton Keynes, 1988

3 Robin Skynner and John Cleese, *Families and How to Survive them*, London, Methuen, 1983, p.247

4 John Powell, *The Christian Vision*, Allen, Texas: Argos Communications, 1984

5 Neil Anderson, *Victory Over the Darkness*, Monarch, 1992

6 Henri Nouwen, *Life of the Beloved*, London: Hodder and Stoughton, 1992

7 Sam Storms, *The Singing God*, Orlando, Fl.: Creation House, 1998

8 Philip Yancey, *Disappointment with God*, London: Marshall Pickering, 1989

9 J.B. Phillips, *Good News*, London: Geoffrey Bles, 1964

10 Richard Wurmbrand, *In God's Underground*, W.H. Allen, 1968

11 Minnie Louise Haskins, *The Desert*, 1908

12 Mary Pytches, *A Father's Place*, London, Hodder and Stoughton, 1993 p.75

13 C.S. Lewis, *The Four Loves*, London: Collins, 1960, p.63

14  Ashley Montagu, *Touching*, New York: Harper & Row, 1971, p.98

15  Victor Frankl, *Man's Search for Meaning*, Beacon Press, 1993

16  Barbara Johnson, *Splashes of Joy in the Cesspools of Life*, Word Pub, 1992

17  Mary Pytches, *Rising Above the Storms of Life*, Eagle Pub., 2000

18  Abe Wagner, *Say it Straight or You'll Show it Crooked*, Industrial Society, 1996 p.123

19  Norman Cousins, *Anatomy of an Illness as Perceived by the Patient*, New York: Norton, 1979

20  Health & Safety Executive, *Health and Safety Statistics, 1996/7*, HSE Books, Sudbury, 1997

21  J.C. Pollock, *Hudson Taylor and Maria*, Hodder and Stoughton, London 1962, p.21

22  F.W. Bourne, *Billy Bray*, Epworth Press, London 1942, p.62

23  John Maxwell, *Developing the Leader Within You*, Thomas Nelson, 1993, p.161

24  John Powell, *Happiness is an Inside Job*, Tabor Pub, 1989, p.5

25  George Malone, *Arming for Spiritual Warfare*, IVP, Illinois, 1991, p.36

26  C.S. Lewis, *The Great Divorce*, Glasgow: William Collins Sons & Co, 1946, p.66

27  Idea taken from *Free To Be Course*, Christian Life Training, 1090 N Batavia, Orange, CA 92867, USA

28  Mary Pytches, *Rising Above the Storms of Life*, Eagle Pub, 2000, p.115

Mary and David Pytches have been part of New Wine since its inception: New Wine grew out of David Pytches' ministry at St Andrew's, Chorleywood. Today's New Wine leadership team are pleased to welcome the publication of this new resource.

## New Wine Vision

We want to see as many Christians and churches as possible alive with the joy of knowing and worshipping Jesus Christ, and equipped to live out and proclaim his Kingdom in the love of God the Father, and the power and gifts of the Holy Spirit.

## New Wine Mission

Through the Holy Spirit, we seek fulfilment of this vision through:

● Summer Family Conferences. These events aim to envision and empower Christians and churches for worship which is passionate, intimate, reverent and biblical; for ministry in the power and gifts of the Spirit, modelled in a mature, responsible way; and through Bible expositions and a breadth of seminar options, to equip them for Spirit-filled Christian life and ministry.

● The work of the New Wine Networks. Providing relational support and encouragement for like-minded leaders across the UK and other nations. Regional training conferences (1-3 days in length) are held all around the networks. We also place strategic emphasis on training church leaders through a programme of leadership training conferences, and the New Wine Leaders' Retreats.

● Encouraging faith-sharing visits to churches that are seeking to grow in renewal by leaders and other teachers taking out teams of people from their churches

● Discerning where the Spirit is leading in issues of social responsibility, justice, community and the environment.

● Encouraging church planting.

● Publishing: New Wine Magazine, books and other teaching materials (e.g. video and audio cassette material) as a further means of propagating teaching which adheres to New Wine values.

In this work we have a special, though not exclusive, concern for the Church of England, from which New Wine emerged, and other traditional churches.

**New Wine** – equipping churches to extend Jesus' Kingdom

New Wine, 4A Ridley Avenue, Ealing, London W13 9XW
Tel. 020 8567 6717    Fax. 020 8840 4735

Email info@new-wine.org
Web Site www.new-wine.org